Think Java
How to Think Like a Computer Scientist

Allen B. Downey and Chris Mayfield

Beijing · Boston · Farnham · Sebastopol · Tokyo

Think Java

by Allen B. Downey and Chris Mayfield

Printed in the United States of America.

Published by O'Reilly Media, Inc., 1005 Gravenstein Highway North, Sebastopol, CA 95472.

O'Reilly books may be purchased for educational, business, or sales promotional use. Online editions are also available for most titles (*http://oreilly.com/safari*). For more information, contact our corporate/institutional sales department: 800-998-9938 or *corporate@oreilly.com*.

Editor: Brian Foster
Production Editor: Kristen Brown
Copyeditor: Charles Roumeliotis
Proofreader: Christina Edwards

Indexers: Allen B. Downey and Chris Mayfield
Interior Designer: David Futato
Cover Designer: Karen Montgomery
Illustrator: Rebecca Demarest

May 2016:   First Edition

Revision History for the First Edition
2016-05-06:   First Release
2017-04-21:   Second Release

See *http://oreilly.com/catalog/errata.csp?isbn=9781491929568* for release details.

978-1-491-92956-8

[LSI]

Table of Contents

Preface

Think Java is an introduction to computer science and programming intended for readers with little or no experience. We start with the most basic concepts and are careful to define all terms when they are first used. The book presents each new idea in a logical progression. Larger topics, like recursion and object-oriented programming, are divided into smaller examples and introduced over the course of several chapters.

This book is intentionally concise. Each chapter is 12–14 pages and covers the material for one week of a college course. It is not meant to be a comprehensive presentation of Java, but rather, an initial exposure to programming constructs and techniques. We begin with small problems and basic algorithms and work up to object-oriented design. In the vocabulary of computer science pedagogy, this book uses the "objects late" approach.

The Philosophy Behind the Book

Here are the guiding principles that make the book the way it is:

- *One concept at a time.* We break down topics that give beginners trouble into a series of small steps, so that they can exercise each new concept in isolation before continuing.

- *Balance of Java and concepts.* The book is not primarily about Java; it uses code examples to demonstrate computer science. Most chapters start with language features and end with concepts.

- *Conciseness.* An important goal of the book is to be small enough so that students can read and understand the entire text in a one-semester college or AP course.

- *Emphasis on vocabulary.* We try to introduce the minimum number of terms and define them carefully when they are first used. We also organize them in glossaries at the end of each chapter.

- *Program development.* There are many strategies for writing programs, including bottom-up, top-down, and others. We demonstrate multiple program development techniques, allowing readers to choose methods that work best for them.

- *Multiple learning curves.* To write a program, you have to understand the algorithm, know the programming language, and be able to debug errors. We discuss these and other aspects throughout the book, and include an appendix that summarizes our advice.

Object-Oriented Programming

Some Java books introduce classes and objects immediately; others begin with procedural programming and transition to object-oriented more gradually.

Many of Java's object-oriented features are motivated by problems with previous languages, and their implementations are influenced by this history. Some of these features are hard to explain when people aren't familiar with the problems they solve.

We get to object-oriented programming as quickly as possible, limited by the requirement that we introduce concepts one at a time, as clearly as possible, in a way that allows readers to practice each idea in isolation before moving on. So it takes some time to get there.

But you can't write Java programs (even hello world) without encountering object-oriented features. In some cases we explain a feature briefly when it first appears, and then explain it more deeply later on.

This book is well suited to prepare students for the AP Computer Science A exam, which includes object-oriented design and implementation. (AP is a registered trademark of the College Board.) We introduce nearly every topic in the "AP Java subset" with a few exceptions. A mapping of *Think Java* section numbers to the current AP course description is available on our website: *http://thinkjava.org.*

Appendixes

The chapters of this book are meant to be read in order, because each one builds on the previous one. We also include three appendixes with material that can be read at any time:

Appendix A, Development Tools

The steps for compiling, running, and debugging Java code depend on the details of the development environment and operating system. We avoided putting these details in the main text, because they can be distracting. Instead, we provide this appendix with a brief introduction to DrJava—an interactive development environment (IDE) that is helpful for beginners—and other development tools, including Checkstyle for code quality and JUnit for testing.

Appendix B, Java 2D Graphics

Java provides libraries for working with graphics and animation, and these topics can be engaging for students. The libraries require object-oriented features that readers will not completely understand until after Chapter 11, but they can be used much earlier.

Appendix C, Debugging

We provide debugging suggestions throughout the book, but we also collect our debugging advice in an appendix. We recommend that readers review this appendix several times as they work through the book.

Using the Code Examples

Most of the code examples in this book are available from a Git repository at *https://github.com/AllenDowney/ThinkJavaCode*. Git is a "version control system" that allows you to keep track of the files that make up a project. A collection of files under Git's control is called a "repository".

GitHub is a hosting service that provides storage for Git repositories and a convenient web interface. It provides several ways to work with the code:

- You can create a copy of the repository on GitHub by pressing the *Fork* button. If you don't already have a GitHub account, you'll need to create one. After forking, you'll have your own repository on GitHub that you can use to keep track of code you write. Then you can "clone" the repository, which downloads a copy of the files to your computer.

- Alternatively, you could clone the repository without forking. If you choose this option, you don't need a GitHub account, but you won't be able to save your changes on GitHub.

- If you don't want to use Git at all, you can download the code in a ZIP archive using the *Download ZIP* button on the GitHub page, or this link: *http://tinyurl.com/ThinkJavaCodeZip*.

After you clone the repository or unzip the ZIP file, you should have a directory called ThinkJavaCode with a subdirectory for each chapter in the book.

All examples in this book were developed and tested using Java SE Development Kit 8. If you are using a more recent version, the examples in this book should still work. If you are using an older version, some of them may not.

Conventions Used in This Book

The following typographical conventions are used in this book:

Italic
> Indicates emphasis, keystrokes, menu options, URLs, and email addresses.

Bold
> Indicates terms defined in the Vocabulary section at the end of each chapter.

`Constant width`
> Used for program listings, as well as within paragraphs to refer to filenames, file extensions, and program elements such as variable and function names, data types, statements, and keywords.

`Constant width bold`
> Shows commands or other text that should be typed literally by the user.

O'Reilly Safari

 Safari (formerly Safari Books Online) is a membership-based training and reference platform for enterprise, government, educators, and individuals.

Members have access to thousands of books, training videos, Learning Paths, interactive tutorials, and curated playlists from over 250 publishers, including O'Reilly Media, Harvard Business Review, Prentice Hall Professional, Addison-Wesley Professional, Microsoft Press, Sams, Que, Peachpit Press, Adobe, Focal Press, Cisco Press, John Wiley & Sons, Syngress, Morgan Kaufmann, IBM Redbooks, Packt, Adobe Press, FT Press, Apress, Manning, New Riders, McGraw-Hill, Jones & Bartlett, and Course Technology, among others.

For more information, please visit *http://oreilly.com/safari*.

How to Contact Us

Please address comments and questions concerning this book to the publisher:

O'Reilly Media, Inc.
1005 Gravenstein Highway North
Sebastopol, CA 95472
800-998-9938 (in the United States or Canada)
707-829-0515 (international or local)
707-829-0104 (fax)

We have a web page for this book, where we list errata, examples, and any additional information. You can access this page at *http://bit.ly/think-java-1e*.

To comment or ask technical questions about this book, send email to *bookquestions@oreilly.com*.

For more information about our books, courses, conferences, and news, see our website at *http://www.oreilly.com*.

Find us on Facebook: *http://facebook.com/oreilly*

Follow us on Twitter: *http://twitter.com/oreillymedia*

Watch us on YouTube: *http://www.youtube.com/oreillymedia*

Acknowledgments

Many people have sent corrections and suggestions, and we appreciate their valuable feedback!

- Ellen Hildreth used this book to teach Data Structures at Wellesley College and submitted a whole stack of corrections, along with some great suggestions.

- Tania Passfield pointed out that some glossaries had leftover terms that no longer appeared in the text.

- Elizabeth Wiethoff noticed that the series expansion of $\exp\left(-x^2\right)$ was wrong. She has also worked on a Ruby version of the book.

- Matt Crawford sent in a whole patch file full of corrections.

- Chi-Yu Li pointed out a typo and an error in one of the code examples.

- Doan Thanh Nam corrected an example.

- Muhammad Saied translated the book into Arabic, and found several errors in the process.

- Marius Margowski found an inconsistency in a code example.

- Leslie Klein discovered another error in the series expansion of $\exp\left(-x^2\right)$, identified typos in the card array figures, and gave helpful suggestions to clarify several exercises.

- Micah Lindstrom reported half a dozen typos and sent corrections.

- James Riely ported the textbook source from LaTeX to Sphinx: *http://fpl.cs.depaul.edu/jriely/thinkapjava/*.

- Peter Knaggs ported the book to C#: *http://www.rigwit.co.uk/think/sharp/*.

- Heidi Gentry-Kolen recorded several video lectures that follow the book: *https://www.youtube.com/user/digipipeline*.

We are especially grateful to our technical reviewers: Blythe Samuels, David Wisneski, and Stephen Rose. They found errors, made many great suggestions, and helped make the book much better.

Additional contributors who found one or more typos: Stijn Debrouwere, Guy Driesen, Andai Velican, Chris Kuszmaul, Daniel Kurikesu, Josh Donath, Rens Findhammer, Elisa Abedrapo, Yousef BaAfif, Bruce Hill, Matt Underwood, Isaac Sultan, Dan Rice, Robert Beard, Daniel Pierce, Michael Giftthaler, and Min Zeng.

If you have additional comments or ideas about the text, please send them to: *feedback@greenteapress.com*.

CHAPTER 1

The Way of the Program

The goal of this book is to teach you to think like a computer scientist. This way of thinking combines some of the best features of mathematics, engineering, and natural science. Like mathematicians, computer scientists use formal languages to denote ideas, specifically computations. Like engineers, they design things, assembling components into systems and evaluating trade-offs among alternatives. And like scientists, they observe the behavior of complex systems, form hypotheses, and test predictions.

The single most important skill for a computer scientist is **problem solving**. It involves the ability to formulate problems, think creatively about solutions, and express solutions clearly and accurately. As it turns out, the process of learning to program is an excellent opportunity to develop problem solving skills. That's why this chapter is called, "The way of the program".

On one level you will be learning to program, a useful skill by itself. But on another level you will use programming as a means to an end. As we go along, that end will become clearer.

What Is Programming?

A **program** is a sequence of instructions that specifies how to perform a computation. The computation might be something mathematical, like solving a system of equations or finding the roots of a polynomial. It can also be a symbolic computation, like searching and replacing text in a document or (strangely enough) compiling a program. The details look different in different languages, but a few basic instructions appear in just about every language.

input:
Get data from the keyboard, a file, a sensor, or some other device.

output:
Display data on the screen, or send data to a file or other device.

math:
Perform basic mathematical operations like addition and division.

decisions:
Check for certain conditions and execute the appropriate code.

repetition:
Perform some action repeatedly, usually with some variation.

Believe it or not, that's pretty much all there is to it. Every program you've ever used, no matter how complicated, is made up of small instructions that look much like these. So you can think of **programming** as the process of breaking down a large, complex task into smaller and smaller subtasks. The process continues until the subtasks are simple enough to be performed with the basic instructions provided by the computer.

What Is Computer Science?

One of the most interesting aspects of writing programs is deciding how to solve a particular problem, especially when there are multiple solutions. For example, there are numerous ways to sort a list of numbers, and each way has its advantages. In order to determine which way is best for a given situation, we need techniques for describing and analyzing solutions formally.

Computer science is the science of algorithms, including their discovery and analysis. An **algorithm** is a sequence of steps that specifies how to solve a problem. Some algorithms are faster than others, and some use less space in computer memory. As you learn to develop algorithms for problems you haven't solved before, you also learn to think like a computer scientist.

Designing algorithms and writing code is difficult and error-prone. For historical reasons, programming errors are called **bugs**, and the process of tracking them down and correcting them is called **debugging**. As you learn to debug your programs, you will develop new problem solving skills. You will need to think creatively when unexpected errors happen.

Although it can be frustrating, debugging is an intellectually rich, challenging, and interesting part of computer programming. In some ways, debugging is like detective work. You are confronted with clues, and you have to infer the processes and events that led to the results you see. Thinking about how to correct programs and improve their performance sometimes even leads to the discovery of new algorithms.

Programming Languages

The programming language you will learn is Java, which is a **high-level language**. Other high-level languages you may have heard of include Python, C and C++, Ruby, and JavaScript.

Before they can run, programs in high-level languages have to be translated into a **low-level language**, also called "machine language". This translation takes some time, which is a small disadvantage of high-level languages. But high-level languages have two advantages:

- It is *much* easier to program in a high-level language. Programs take less time to write, they are shorter and easier to read, and they are more likely to be correct.
- High-level languages are **portable**, meaning they can run on different kinds of computers with few or no modifications. Low-level programs can only run on one kind of computer, and have to be rewritten to run on another.

Two kinds of programs translate high-level languages into low-level languages: interpreters and compilers. An **interpreter** reads a high-level program and executes it, meaning that it does what the program says. It processes the program a little at a time, alternately reading lines and performing computations. Figure 1-1 shows the structure of an interpreter.

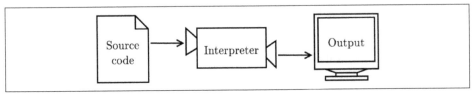

Figure 1-1. How interpreted languages are executed.

In contrast, a **compiler** reads the entire program and translates it completely before the program starts running. In this context, the high-level program is called the **source code**, and the translated program is called the **object code** or the **executable**. Once a program is compiled, you can execute it repeatedly without further translation. As a result, compiled programs often run faster than interpreted programs.

Java is *both* compiled and interpreted. Instead of translating programs directly into machine language, the Java compiler generates **byte code**. Similar to machine language, byte code is easy and fast to interpret. But it is also portable, so it is possible to compile a Java program on one machine, transfer the byte code to another machine, and run the byte code on the other machine. The interpreter that runs byte code is called a "Java Virtual Machine" (JVM).

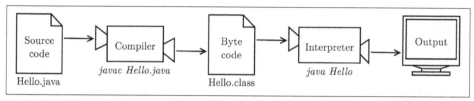

Figure 1-2. The process of compiling and running a Java program.

Figure 1-2 shows the steps of this process. Although it might seem complicated, these steps are automated for you in most program development environments. Usually you only have to press a button or type a single command to compile and run your program. On the other hand, it is important to know what steps are happening in the background, so if something goes wrong you can figure out what it is.

The Hello World Program

Traditionally, the first program you write when learning a new programming language is called the hello world program. All it does is display the words "Hello, World!" on the screen. In Java, it looks like this:

```
public class Hello {

    public static void main(String[] args) {
        // generate some simple output
        System.out.println("Hello, World!");
    }
}
```

When this program runs it displays:

```
Hello, World!
```

Notice that the output does not include the quotation marks.

Java programs are made up of *class* and *method* definitions, and methods are made up of *statements*. A **statement** is a line of code that performs a basic operation. In the hello world program, this line is a **print statement** that displays a message on the screen:

```
System.out.println("Hello, World!");
```

`System.out.println` displays results on the screen; the name `println` stands for "print line". Confusingly, *print* can mean both "display on the screen" and "send to the printer". In this book, we'll try to say "display" when we mean output to the screen. Like most statements, the print statement ends with a semicolon (;).

Java is "case-sensitive", which means that uppercase and lowercase are not the same. In this example, System has to begin with an uppercase letter; system and SYSTEM won't work.

A **method** is a named sequence of statements. This program defines one method named main:

```
public static void main(String[] args)
```

The name and format of main is special: when the program runs, it starts at the first statement in main and ends when it finishes the last statement. Later, we will see programs that define more than one method.

A **class** is a collection of methods. This program defines a class named Hello. You can give a class any name you like, but it is conventional to start with a capital letter. The name of the class has to match the name of the file it is in, so this class has to be in a file named Hello.java.

Java uses squiggly braces ({ and }) to group things together. In Hello.java, the outermost braces contain the class definition, and the inner braces contain the method definition.

The line that begins with two slashes (//) is a **comment**, which is a bit of English text that explains the code. When the compiler sees //, it ignores everything from there until the end of the line. Comments have no effect on the execution of the program, but they make it easier for other programmers (and your future self) to understand what you meant to do.

Displaying Strings

You can put as many statements as you like in main. For example, to display more than one line of output:

```
public class Hello {

    public static void main(String[] args) {
        // generate some simple output
        System.out.println("Hello, World!");  // first line
        System.out.println("How are you?");   // another line
    }
}
```

As this example shows, you can put comments at the end of a line as well as on lines all by themselves.

Phrases that appear in quotation marks are called **strings**, because they contain a sequence of "characters" strung together. Characters can be letters, numbers, punctuation marks, symbols, spaces, tabs, etc.

`System.out.println` appends a special character, called a **newline**, that moves to the beginning of the next line. If you don't want a newline at the end, you can use `print` instead of `println`:

```
public class Goodbye {

    public static void main(String[] args) {
        System.out.print("Goodbye, ");
        System.out.println("cruel world");
    }
}
```

In this example, the first statement does not add a newline, so the output appears on a single line as Goodbye, cruel world. Notice that there is a space at the end of the first string, which appears in the output.

Escape Sequences

It is possible to display multiple lines of output in just one line of code. You just have to tell Java where to put the line breaks.

```
public class Hello {

    public static void main(String[] args) {
        System.out.print("Hello!\nHow are you doing?\n");
    }
}
```

The output is two lines, each ending with a newline character:

```
Hello!
How are you doing?
```

The \n is an **escape sequence**, which is a sequence of characters that represents a special character. The backslash allows you to "escape" the string's literal interpretation. Notice there is no space between \n and How. If you add a space there, there will be a space at the beginning of the second line.

Another common use of escape sequences is to have quotation marks inside of strings. Since double quotes indicate the beginning and end of strings, you need to escape them with a backslash.

```
System.out.println("She said \"Hello!\" to me.");
```

The result is:

```
She said "Hello!" to me.
```

Table 1-1. Common escape sequences

\n	newline
\t	tab
\"	double quote
\\	backslash

Formatting Code

In Java programs, some spaces are required. For example, you need at least one space between words, so this program is not legal:

```
publicclassGoodbye{

    publicstaticvoidmain(String[] args) {
        System.out.print("Goodbye, ");
        System.out.println("cruel world");
    }
}
```

But most other spaces are optional. For example, this program is legal:

```
public class Goodbye {
public static void main(String[] args) {
System.out.print("Goodbye, ");
System.out.println("cruel world");
}
}
```

The newlines are optional, too. So we could just write:

```
public class Goodbye { public static void main(String[] args)
{ System.out.print("Goodbye, "); System.out.println
("cruel world");}}
```

It still works, but the program is getting harder and harder to read. Newlines and spaces are important for organizing your program visually, making it easier to understand the program and find errors when they occur.

Many editors will automatically format source code with consistent indenting and line breaks. For example, in DrJava (see Appendix A) you can indent the code by selecting all text (*Ctrl+A*) and pressing the *Tab* key.

Organizations that do a lot of software development usually have strict guidelines on how to format source code. For example, Google publishes its Java coding standards for use in open-source projects: *http://google.github.io/styleguide/javaguide.html*.

You might not understand these guidelines now, because they refer to language features we haven't yet seen. But you might want to refer back to them periodically as you read this book.

Debugging Code

It is a good idea to read this book in front of a computer so you can try out the examples as you go. You can run many of the examples directly in DrJava's Interactions Pane (see Appendix A). But if you put the code in a source file, it will be easier to try out variations.

Whenever you are experimenting with a new feature, you should also try to make mistakes. For example, in the hello world program, what happens if you leave out one of the quotation marks? What if you leave out both? What if you spell `println` wrong? These kinds of experiments help you remember what you read. They also help with debugging, because you learn what the error messages mean. It is better to make mistakes now and on purpose than later on and accidentally.

Debugging is like an experimental science: once you have an idea about what is going wrong, you modify your program and try again. If your hypothesis was correct, then you can predict the result of the modification, and you take a step closer to a working program. If your hypothesis was wrong, you have to come up with a new one.

Programming and debugging should go hand in hand. Don't just write a bunch of code and then perform trial and error debugging until it all works. Instead, start with a program that does *something* and make small modifications, debugging them as you go, until the program does what you want. That way you will always have a working program, and it will be easier to isolate errors.

A great example of this principle is the Linux operating system, which contains millions of lines of code. It started out as a simple program Linus Torvalds used to explore the Intel 80386 chip. According to Larry Greenfield in *The Linux Users' Guide*, "One of Linus's earlier projects was a program that would switch between printing AAAA and BBBB. This later evolved to Linux."

Finally, programming sometimes brings out strong emotions. If you are struggling with a difficult bug, you might feel angry, despondent, or embarrassed. Remember that you are not alone, and most if not all programmers have had similar experiences. Don't hesitate to reach out to a friend and ask questions!

Vocabulary

Throughout the book, we try to define each term the first time we use it. At the end of each chapter, we include the new terms and their definitions in order of appearance.

If you spend some time learning this vocabulary, you will have an easier time reading the following chapters.

problem solving:
> The process of formulating a problem, finding a solution, and expressing the solution.

program:
> A sequence of instructions that specifies how to perform tasks on a computer.

programming:
> The application of problem solving to creating executable computer programs.

computer science:
> The scientific and practical approach to computation and its applications.

algorithm:
> A procedure or formula for solving a problem, with or without a computer.

bug:
> An error in a program.

debugging:
> The process of finding and removing errors.

high-level language:
> A programming language that is designed to be easy for humans to read and write.

low-level language:
> A programming language that is designed to be easy for a computer to run. Also called "machine language" or "assembly language".

portable:
> The ability of a program to run on more than one kind of computer.

interpret:
> To run a program in a high-level language by translating it one line at a time and immediately executing the corresponding instructions.

compile:
> To translate a program in a high-level language into a low-level language, all at once, in preparation for later execution.

source code:
> A program in a high-level language, before being compiled.

object code:

The output of the compiler, after translating the program.

executable:

Another name for object code that is ready to run on specific hardware.

byte code:

A special kind of object code used for Java programs. Byte code is similar to a low-level language, but it is portable like a high-level language.

statement:

Part of a program that specifies one step of an algorithm.

print statement:

A statement that causes output to be displayed on the screen.

method:

A named sequence of statements.

class:

For now, a collection of related methods. (We will see later that there is more to it.)

comment:

A part of a program that contains information about the program but has no effect when the program runs.

string:

A sequence of characters; the primary data type for text.

newline:

A special character signifying the end of a line of text. Also known as line ending, end of line (EOL), or line break.

escape sequence:

A sequence of code that represents a special character when used inside a string.

Exercises

At the end of each chapter, we include exercises you can do with the things you've learned. We encourage you to at least attempt every problem. You can't learn to program only by reading about it; you have to practice.

Before you can compile and run Java programs, you might have to download and install a few tools. There are many good options, but we recommend DrJava, which is an "integrated development environment" (IDE) well suited for beginners. Instructions for getting started are in "Installing DrJava" on page 201.

The code for this chapter is in the ch01 directory of ThinkJavaCode. See "Using the Code Examples" on page xi for instructions on how to download the repository. Before you start the exercises, we recommend that you compile and run the examples.

Exercise 1-1.

Computer scientists have the annoying habit of using common English words to mean something other than their common English meaning. For example, in English, statements and comments are the same thing, but in programs they are different.

1. In computer jargon, what's the difference between a statement and a comment?
2. What does it mean to say that a program is portable?
3. In common English, what does the word compile mean?
4. What is an executable? Why is that word used as a noun?

The glossary at the end of each chapter is intended to highlight words and phrases that have special meanings in computer science. When you see familiar words, don't assume that you know what they mean!

Exercise 1-2.

Before you do anything else, find out how to compile and run a Java program. Some environments provide sample programs similar to the example in "The Hello World Program" on page 4.

1. Type in the hello world program, then compile and run it.
2. Add a print statement that displays a second message after the "Hello, World!". Say something witty like, "How are you?" Compile and run the program again.
3. Add a comment to the program (anywhere), recompile, and run it again. The new comment should not affect the result.

This exercise may seem trivial, but it is the starting place for many of the programs we will work with. To debug with confidence, you will need to have confidence in your programming environment.

In some environments, it is easy to lose track of which program is executing. You might find yourself trying to debug one program while you are accidentally running another. Adding (and changing) print statements is a simple way to be sure that the program you are looking at is the program you are running.

Exercise 1-3.

It is a good idea to commit as many errors as you can think of, so that you see what error messages the compiler produces. Sometimes the compiler tells you exactly what is wrong, and all you have to do is fix it. But sometimes the error messages are misleading. Over time you will develop a sense for when you can trust the compiler and when you have to figure things out yourself.

Starting with the hello world program, try out each of the following errors. After you make each change, compile the program, read the error message (if there is one), and then fix the error.

1. Remove one of the open squiggly braces.
2. Remove one of the close squiggly braces.
3. Instead of `main`, write `mian`.
4. Remove the word `static`.
5. Remove the word `public`.
6. Remove the word `System`.
7. Replace `println` with `Println`.
8. Replace `println` with `print`.
9. Delete one of the parentheses. Add an extra one.

CHAPTER 2

Variables and Operators

This chapter describes how to write statements using variables, which store values like numbers and words, and operators, which are symbols that perform a computation. We also explain three kinds of programming errors and offer additional debugging advice.

Declaring Variables

One of the most powerful features of a programming language is the ability to define and manipulate **variables**. A variable is a named location that stores a **value**. Values may be numbers, text, images, sounds, and other types of data. To store a value, you first have to declare a variable.

```
String message;
```

This statement is a **declaration**, because it declares that the variable named message has the type String. Each variable has a **type** that determines what kind of values it can store. For example, the int type can store integers, and the char type can store characters.

Some types begin with a capital letter and some with lowercase. We will learn the significance of this distinction later, but for now you should take care to get it right. There is no such type as Int or string.

To declare an integer variable named x, you simply type:

```
int x;
```

Note that x is an arbitrary name for the variable. In general, you should use names that indicate what the variables mean. For example, if you saw these declarations, you could probably guess what values would be stored:

```
String firstName;
String lastName;
int hour, minute;
```

This example declares two variables with type String and two with type int. When a variable name contains more than one word, like firstName, it is conventional to capitalize the first letter of each word except the first. Variable names are case-sensitive, so firstName is not the same as firstname or FirstName.

This example also demonstrates the **syntax** for declaring multiple variables with the same type on one line: hour and minute are both integers. Note that each declaration statement ends with a semicolon.

You can use any name you want for a variable. But there are about 50 reserved words, called **keywords**, that you are not allowed to use as variable names. These words include public, class, static, void, and int, which are used by the compiler to analyze the structure of the program.

You can find the complete list of keywords at *http://docs.oracle.com/javase/tutorial/ java/nutsandbolts/_keywords.html*, but you don't have to memorize them. Most programming editors provide "syntax highlighting", which makes different parts of the program appear in different colors.

Assignment

Now that we have declared variables, we want to use them to store values. We do that with an **assignment** statement.

```
message = "Hello!";   // give message the value "Hello!"
hour = 11;            // assign the value 11 to hour
minute = 59;          // set minute to 59
```

This example shows three assignments, and the comments illustrate different ways people sometimes talk about assignment statements. The vocabulary can be confusing here, but the idea is straightforward:

- When you declare a variable, you create a named storage location.
- When you make an assignment to a variable, you update its value.

As a general rule, a variable has to have the same type as the value you assign to it. For example, you cannot store a string in minute or an integer in message. We will see some examples that seem to break this rule, but we'll get to that later.

A common source of confusion is that some strings *look* like integers, but they are not. For example, message can contain the string "123", which is made up of the characters '1', '2', and '3'. But that is not the same thing as the integer 123.

```
message = "123";      // legal
message = 123;        // not legal
```

Variables must be **initialized** (assigned for the first time) before they can be used. You can declare a variable and then assign a value later, as in the previous example. You can also declare and initialize on the same line:

```
String message = "Hello!";
int hour = 11;
int minute = 59;
```

State Diagrams

Because Java uses the = symbol for assignment, it is tempting to interpret the statement a = b as a statement of equality. It is not!

Equality is commutative, and assignment is not. For example, in mathematics if $a = 7$ then $7 = a$. In Java a = 7; is a legal assignment statement, but 7 = a; is not. The left side of an assignment statement has to be a variable name (storage location).

Also, in mathematics, a statement of equality is true for all time. If $a = b$ now, a is always equal to b. In Java, an assignment statement can make two variables equal, but they don't have to stay that way.

```
int a = 5;
int b = a;    // a and b are now equal
a = 3;        // a and b are no longer equal
```

The third line changes the value of a, but it does not change the value of b, so they are no longer equal.

Taken together, the variables in a program and their current values make up the program's **state**. Figure 2-1 shows the state of the program after these assignment statements run.

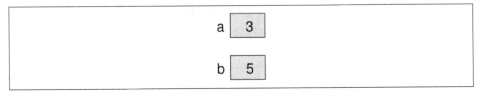

Figure 2-1. State diagram of the variables a and b.

Diagrams like this one that show the state of the program are called **state diagrams**. Each variable is represented with a box showing the name of the variable on the outside and the value inside. As the program runs, the state changes, so you should think of a state diagram as a snapshot of a particular point in time.

Printing Variables

You can display the value of a variable using `print` or `println`. The following statements declare a variable named `firstLine`, assign it the value `"Hello, again!"`, and display that value.

```
String firstLine = "Hello, again!";
System.out.println(firstLine);
```

When we talk about displaying a variable, we generally mean the *value* of the variable. To display the *name* of a variable, you have to put it in quotes.

```
System.out.print("The value of firstLine is ");
System.out.println(firstLine);
```

For this example, the output is:

```
The value of firstLine is Hello, again!
```

Conveniently, the syntax for displaying a variable is the same regardless of its type. For example:

```
int hour = 11;
int minute = 59;
System.out.print("The current time is ");
System.out.print(hour);
System.out.print(":");
System.out.print(minute);
System.out.println(".");
```

The output of this program is:

```
The current time is 11:59.
```

To output multiple values on the same line, it's common to use several `print` statements followed by `println` at the end. But don't forget the `println`! On many computers, the output from `print` is stored without being displayed until `println` is run; then the entire line is displayed at once. If you omit the `println`, the program might display the stored output at unexpected times or even terminate without displaying anything.

Arithmetic Operators

Operators are symbols that represent simple computations. For example, the addition operator is +, subtraction is -, multiplication is *, and division is /.

The following program converts a time of day to minutes:

```
int hour = 11;
int minute = 59;
System.out.print("Number of minutes since midnight: ");
System.out.println(hour * 60 + minute);
```

In this program, hour * 60 + minute is an **expression**, which represents a single value to be computed. When the program runs, each variable is replaced by its current value, and then the operators are applied. The values operators work with are called **operands**.

The result of the previous example is:

```
Number of minutes since midnight: 719
```

Expressions are generally a combination of numbers, variables, and operators. When complied and executed, they become a single value.

For example, the expression 1 + 1 has the value 2. In the expression hour - 1, Java replaces the variable with its value, yielding 11 - 1, which has the value 10. In the expression hour * 60 + minute, both variables get replaced, yielding 11 * 60 + 59. The multiplication happens first, yielding 660 + 59. Then the addition yields 719.

Addition, subtraction, and multiplication all do what you expect, but you might be surprised by division. For example, the following fragment tries to compute the fraction of an hour that has elapsed:

```
System.out.print("Fraction of the hour that has passed: ");
System.out.println(minute / 60);
```

The output is:

```
Fraction of the hour that has passed: 0
```

This result often confuses people. The value of minute is 59, and 59 divided by 60 should be 0.98333, not 0. The problem is that Java performs "integer division" when the operands are integers. By design, integer division always rounds toward zero, even in cases like this one where the next integer is close.

As an alternative, we can calculate a percentage rather than a fraction:

```
System.out.print("Percent of the hour that has passed: ");
System.out.println(minute * 100 / 60);
```

The new output is:

```
Percent of the hour that has passed: 98
```

Again the result is rounded down, but at least now it's approximately correct.

Floating-Point Numbers

A more general solution is to use **floating-point** numbers, which can represent fractions as well as integers. In Java, the default floating-point type is called double, which is short for double-precision. You can create double variables and assign values to them using the same syntax we used for the other types:

```
double pi;
pi = 3.14159;
```

Java performs "floating-point division" when one or more operands are `double` values. So we can solve the problem we saw in the previous section:

```
double minute = 59.0;
System.out.print("Fraction of the hour that has passed: ");
System.out.println(minute / 60.0);
```

The output is:

```
Fraction of the hour that has passed: 0.9833333333333333
```

Although floating-point numbers are useful, they can be a source of confusion. For example, Java distinguishes the integer value 1 from the floating-point value 1.0, even though they seem to be the same number. They belong to different data types, and strictly speaking, you are not allowed to make assignments between types.

The following is illegal because the variable on the left is an `int` and the value on the right is a `double`:

```
int x = 1.1;  // compiler error
```

It is easy to forget this rule because in many cases Java *automatically* converts from one type to another:

```
double y = 1;  // legal, but bad style
```

The preceding example should be illegal, but Java allows it by converting the `int` value 1 to the `double` value 1.0 automatically. This leniency is convenient, but it often causes problems for beginners. For example:

```
double y = 1 / 3;  // common mistake
```

You might expect the variable y to get the value 0.333333, which is a legal floating-point value. But instead it gets the value 0.0. The expression on the right divides two integers, so Java does integer division, which yields the `int` value 0. Converted to double, the value assigned to y is 0.0.

One way to solve this problem (once you figure out the bug) is to make the right-hand side a floating-point expression. The following sets y to 0.333333, as expected:

```
double y = 1.0 / 3.0;  // correct
```

As a matter of style, you should always assign floating-point values to floating-point variables. The compiler won't make you do it, but you never know when a simple mistake will come back and haunt you.

Rounding Errors

Most floating-point numbers are only *approximately* correct. Some numbers, like reasonably-sized integers, can be represented exactly. But repeating fractions, like 1/3, and irrational numbers, like π, cannot. To represent these numbers, computers have to round off to the nearest floating-point number.

The difference between the number we want and the floating-point number we get is called **rounding error**. For example, the following two statements should be equivalent:

```
System.out.println(0.1 * 10);
System.out.println(0.1 + 0.1 + 0.1 + 0.1 + 0.1
                 + 0.1 + 0.1 + 0.1 + 0.1 + 0.1);
```

But on many machines, the output is:

```
1.0
0.9999999999999999
```

The problem is that `0.1`, which is a terminating fraction in decimal, is a repeating fraction in binary. So its floating-point representation is only approximate. When we add up the approximations, the rounding errors accumulate.

For many applications, like computer graphics, encryption, statistical analysis, and multimedia rendering, floating-point arithmetic has benefits that outweigh the costs. But if you need *absolute* precision, use integers instead. For example, consider a bank account with a balance of $123.45:

```
double balance = 123.45;  // potential rounding error
```

In this example, balances will become inaccurate over time as the variable is used in arithmetic operations like deposits and withdrawals. The result would be angry customers and potential lawsuits. You can avoid the problem by representing the balance as an integer:

```
int balance = 12345;     // total number of cents
```

This solution works as long as the number of cents doesn't exceed the largest integer, which is about 2 billion.

Operators for Strings

In general, you cannot perform mathematical operations on strings, even if the strings look like numbers. The following expressions are illegal:

```
"Hello" - 1     "World" / 123     "Hello" * "World"
```

The + operator works with strings, but it might not do what you expect. For strings, the + operator performs **concatenation**, which means joining end-to-end. So "Hello, " + "World!" yields the string "Hello, World!".

Or if you have a variable called name that has type String, the expression "Hello, " + name appends the value of name to the hello string, which creates a personalized greeting.

Since addition is defined for both numbers and strings, Java performs automatic conversions you may not expect:

```
System.out.println(1 + 2 + "Hello");
// the output is 3Hello

System.out.println("Hello" + 1 + 2);
// the output is Hello12
```

Java executes these operations from left to right. In the first line, 1 + 2 is 3, and 3 + "Hello" is "3Hello". But in the second line, "Hello" + 1 is "Hello1", and "Hello1" + 2 is "Hello12".

When more than one operator appears in an expression, they are evaluated according to **order of operations**. Generally speaking, Java evaluates operators from left to right (as we saw in the previous section). But for numeric operators, Java follows mathematical conventions:

- Multiplication and division take "precedence" over addition and subtraction, which means they happen first. So 1 + 2 * 3 yields 7, not 9, and 2 + 4 / 2 yields 4, not 3.

- If the operators have the same precedence, they are evaluated from left to right. So in the expression minute * 100 / 60, the multiplication happens first; if the value of minute is 59, we get 5900 / 60, which yields 98. If these same operations had gone from right to left, the result would have been 59 * 1, which is incorrect.

- Any time you want to override the order of operations (or you are not sure what it is) you can use parentheses. Expressions in parentheses are evaluated first, so (1 + 2) * 3 is 9. You can also use parentheses to make an expression easier to read, as in (minute * 100) / 60, even though it doesn't change the result.

Don't work too hard to remember the order of operations, especially for other operators. If it's not obvious by looking at the expression, use parentheses to make it clear.

Composition

So far we have looked at the elements of a programming language—variables, expressions, and statements—in isolation, without talking about how to put them together.

One of the most useful features of programming languages is their ability to take small building blocks and **compose** them. For example, we know how to multiply numbers and we know how to display values. We can combine these operations into a single statement:

```
System.out.println(17 * 3);
```

Any arithmetic expression can be used inside a print statement. We've already seen one example:

```
System.out.println(hour * 60 + minute);
```

You can also put arbitrary expressions on the right side of an assignment:

```
int percentage;
percentage = (minute * 100) / 60;
```

The left side of an assignment must be a variable name, not an expression. That's because the left side indicates where the result will be stored, and expressions do not represent storage locations.

```
hour = minute + 1;   // correct
minute + 1 = hour;   // compiler error
```

The ability to compose operations may not seem impressive now, but we will see examples later on that allow us to write complex computations neatly and concisely. But don't get too carried away. Large, complex expressions can be hard to read and debug.

Types of Errors

Three kinds of errors can occur in a program: compile-time errors, run-time errors, and logic errors. It is useful to distinguish among them in order to track them down more quickly.

Compile-time errors occur when you violate the syntax rules of the Java language. For example, parentheses and braces have to come in matching pairs. So (1 + 2) is legal, but 8) is not. In the latter case, the program cannot be compiled, and the compiler displays an error.

Error messages from the compiler usually indicate where in the program the error occurred, and sometimes they can tell you exactly what the error is. As an example, let's get back to the hello world program from "The Hello World Program" on page 4.

```
public class Hello {

    public static void main(String[] args) {
        // generate some simple output
        System.out.println("Hello, World!");
    }
}
```

If you forget the semicolon at the end of the print statement, you might get an error message like this:

```
File: Hello.java  [line: 5]
Error: ';' expected
```

That's pretty good: the location of the error is correct, and the error message tells you what's wrong.

But error messages are not always easy to understand. Sometimes the compiler reports the place in the program where the error was detected, not where it actually occurred. And sometimes the description of the problem is more confusing than helpful.

For example, if you leave out the closing brace at the end of main (line 6), you might get a message like this:

```
File: Hello.java  [line: 7]
Error: reached end of file while parsing
```

There are two problems here. First, the error message is written from the compiler's point of view, not yours. **Parsing** is the process of reading a program before translating; if the compiler gets to the end of the file while still parsing, that means something was omitted. But the compiler doesn't know what. It also doesn't know where. The compiler discovers the error at the end of the program (line 7), but the missing brace should be on the previous line.

Error messages contain useful information, so you should make an effort to read and understand them. But don't take them too literally.

During the first few weeks of your programming career, you will probably spend a lot of time tracking down compile-time errors. But as you gain experience, you will make fewer mistakes and find them more quickly.

The second type of error is a **run-time error**, so-called because it does not appear until after the program has started running. In Java, these errors occur while the interpreter is executing byte code and something goes wrong. These errors are also called "exceptions" because they usually indicate that something exceptional (and bad) has happened.

Run-time errors are rare in the simple programs you will see in the first few chapters, so it might be a while before you encounter one. When a run-time error occurs, the interpreter displays an error message that explains what happened and where.

For example, if you accidentally divide by zero you will get a message like this:

```
Exception in thread "main" java.lang.ArithmeticException: / by zero
    at Hello.main(Hello.java:5)
```

Some parts of this output are useful for debugging. The first line includes the name of the exception, java.lang.ArithmeticException, and a message that indicates more specifically what happened, / by zero. The next line shows the method where the error occurred; Hello.main indicates the method main in the class Hello. It also reports the file where the method is defined, Hello.java, and the line number where the error occurred, 5.

Error messages sometimes contain additional information that won't make sense yet. So one of the challenges is to figure out where to find the useful parts without being overwhelmed by extraneous information. Also, keep in mind that the line where the program crashed may not be the line that needs to be corrected.

The third type of error is the **logic error**. If your program has a logic error, it will compile and run without generating error messages, but it will not do the right thing. Instead, it will do exactly what you told it to do. For example, here is a version of the hello world program with a logic error:

```
public class Hello {

    public static void main(String[] args) {
        System.out.println("Hello, ");
        System.out.println("World!");
    }
}
```

This program compiles and runs just fine, but the output is:

```
Hello,
World!
```

Assuming that we wanted the output on one line, this is not correct. The problem is that the first line uses println, when we probably meant to use print (see the "good-bye world" example of "Displaying Strings" on page 5).

Identifying logic errors can be hard because you have to work backwards, looking at the output of the program, trying to figure out why it is doing the wrong thing, and how to make it do the right thing. Usually the compiler and the interpreter can't help you, since they don't know what the right thing is.

Now that you know about the three kinds of errors, you might want to read Appendix C, where we've collected some of our favorite debugging advice. It refers to language features we haven't talked about yet, so you might want to re-read it from time to time.

Vocabulary

variable:
A named storage location for values. All variables have a type, which is declared when the variable is created.

value:
A number, string, or other data that can be stored in a variable. Every value belongs to a type (for example, `int` or `String`).

declaration:
A statement that creates a new variable and specifies its type.

type:
Mathematically speaking, a set of values. The type of a variable determines which values it can have.

syntax:
The structure of a program; the arrangement of the words and symbols it contains.

keyword:
A reserved word used by the compiler to analyze programs. You cannot use keywords (like `public`, `class`, and `void`) as variable names.

assignment:
A statement that gives a value to a variable.

initialize:
To assign a variable for the first time.

state:
The variables in a program and their current values.

state diagram:
A graphical representation of the state of a program at a point in time.

operator:
A symbol that represents a computation like addition, multiplication, or string concatenation.

operand:
One of the values on which an operator operates. Most operators in Java require two operands.

expression:
> A combination of variables, operators, and values that represents a single value. Expressions also have types, as determined by their operators and operands.

floating-point:
> A data type that represents numbers with an integer part and a fractional part. In Java, the default floating-point type is `double`.

rounding error:
> The difference between the number we want to represent and the nearest floating-point number.

concatenate:
> To join two values, often strings, end-to-end.

order of operations:
> The rules that determine in what order operations are evaluated.

composition:
> The ability to combine simple expressions and statements into compound expressions and statements.

compile-time error:
> An error in the source code that makes it impossible to compile. Also called a "syntax error".

parse:
> To analyze the structure of a program; what the compiler does first.

run-time error:
> An error in a program that makes it impossible to run to completion. Also called an "exception".

logic error:
> An error in a program that makes it do something other than what the programmer intended.

Exercises

The code for this chapter is in the `ch02` directory of `ThinkJavaCode`. See "Using the Code Examples" on page xi for instructions on how to download the repository. Before you start the exercises, we recommend that you compile and run the examples.

If you have not already read "DrJava Interactions" on page 202, now might be a good time. It describes the DrJava Interactions Pane, which is a useful way to develop and test short fragments of code without writing a complete class definition.

Exercise 2-1.

If you are using this book in a class, you might enjoy this exercise. Find a partner and play "Stump the Chump":

Start with a program that compiles and runs correctly. One player looks away while the other player adds an error to the program. Then the first player tries to find and fix the error. You get two points if you find the error without compiling the program, one point if you find it using the compiler, and your opponent gets a point if you don't find it.

Exercise 2-2.

The point of this exercise is (1) to use string concatenation to display values with different types (int and String), and (2) to practice developing programs gradually by adding a few statements at a time.

1. Create a new program named Date.java. Copy or type in something like the hello world program and make sure you can compile and run it.

2. Following the example in "Printing Variables" on page 16, write a program that creates variables named day, date, month, and year. The variable day will contain the day of the week (like Friday), and date will contain the day of the month (like the 13th). What type is each variable? Assign values to those variables that represent today's date.

3. Display (print out) the value of each variable on a line by itself. This is an intermediate step that is useful for checking that everything is working so far. Compile and run your program before moving on.

4. Modify the program so that it displays the date in standard American format, for example: Thursday, July 16, 2015.

5. Modify the program so it also displays the date in European format. The final output should be:

```
American format:
Thursday, July 16, 2015
European format:
Thursday 16 July 2015
```

Exercise 2-3.

The point of this exercise is to (1) use some of the arithmetic operators, and (2) start thinking about compound entities (like time of day) that are represented with multiple values.

1. Create a new program called `Time.java`. From now on, we won't remind you to start with a small, working program, but you should.

2. Following the example program in "Printing Variables" on page 16, create variables named `hour`, `minute`, and `second`. Assign values that are roughly the current time. Use a 24-hour clock so that at 2pm the value of `hour` is 14.

3. Make the program calculate and display the number of seconds since midnight.

4. Calculate and display the number of seconds remaining in the day.

5. Calculate and display the percentage of the day that has passed. You might run into problems when computing percentages with integers, so consider using floating-point.

6. Change the values of `hour`, `minute`, and `second` to reflect the current time. Then write code to compute the elapsed time since you started working on this exercise.

Hint: You might want to use additional variables to hold values during the computation. Variables that are used in a computation but never displayed are sometimes called "intermediate" or "temporary" variables.

CHAPTER 3

Input and Output

The programs we've looked at so far simply display messages, which doesn't involve a lot of real computation. This chapter will show you how to read input from the keyboard, use that input to calculate a result, and then format that result for output.

The System Class

We have been using `System.out.println` for a while, but you might not have thought about what it means. `System` is a class that provides methods related to the "system" or environment where programs run. It also provides `System.out`, which is a special value that provides methods for displaying output, including `println`.

In fact, we can use `System.out.println` to display the value of `System.out`:

```
System.out.println(System.out);
```

The result is:

```
java.io.PrintStream@685d72cd
```

This output indicates that `System.out` is a `PrintStream`, which is defined in a package called `java.io`. A **package** is a collection of related classes; `java.io` contains classes for "I/O" which stands for input and output.

The numbers and letters after the @ sign are the **address** of `System.out`, represented as a hexadecimal (base 16) number. The address of a value is its location in the computer's memory, which might be different on different computers. In this example the address is `685d72cd`, but if you run the same code you might get something different.

As shown in Figure 3-1, `System` is defined in a file called `System.java`, and `Print Stream` is defined in `PrintStream.java`. These files are part of the Java **library**, which is an extensive collection of classes you can use in your programs.

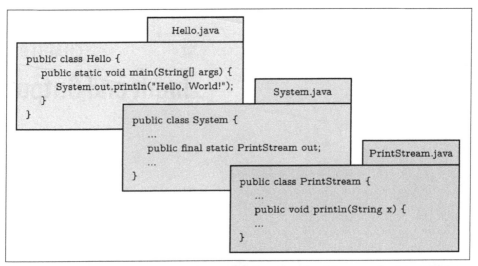

Figure 3-1. System.out.println refers to the out variable of the System class, which is a PrintStream that provides a method called println.

The Scanner Class

The System class also provides the special value System.in, which is an InputStream that provides methods for reading input from the keyboard. These methods are not easy to use; fortunately, Java provides other classes that make it easier to handle common input tasks.

For example, Scanner is a class that provides methods for inputting words, numbers, and other data. Scanner is provided by java.util, which is a package that contains classes so useful they are called "utility classes". Before you can use Scanner, you have to import it like this:

```
import java.util.Scanner;
```

This **import statement** tells the compiler that when you say Scanner, you mean the one defined in java.util. It's necessary because there might be another class named Scanner in another package. Using an import statement makes your code unambiguous.

Import statements can't be inside a class definition. By convention, they are usually at the beginning of the file.

Next you have to create a Scanner:

```
Scanner in = new Scanner(System.in);
```

This line declares a Scanner variable named in and creates a new Scanner that takes input from System.in.

Scanner provides a method called nextLine that reads a line of input from the keyboard and returns a String. The following example reads two lines and repeats them back to the user:

```
import java.util.Scanner;

public class Echo {

    public static void main(String[] args) {
        String line;
        Scanner in = new Scanner(System.in);

        System.out.print("Type something: ");
        line = in.nextLine();
        System.out.println("You said: " + line);

        System.out.print("Type something else: ");
        line = in.nextLine();
        System.out.println("You also said: " + line);
    }
}
```

If you omit the import statement and later refer to Scanner, you will get a compiler error like "cannot find symbol". That means the compiler doesn't know what you mean by Scanner.

You might wonder why we can use the System class without importing it. System belongs to the java.lang package, which is imported automatically. According to the documentation, java.lang "provides classes that are fundamental to the design of the Java programming language." The String class is also part of the java.lang package.

Program Structure

At this point, we have seen all of the elements that make up Java programs. Figure 3-2 shows these organizational units.

To review, a package is a collection of classes, which define methods. Methods contain statements, some of which contain expressions. Expressions are made up of **tokens**, which are the basic elements of a program, including numbers, variable names, operators, keywords, and punctuation like parentheses, braces and semicolons.

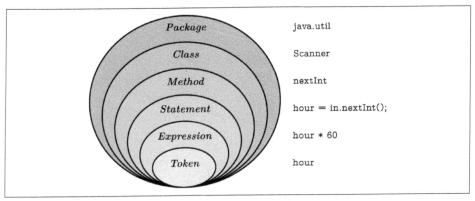

Figure 3-2. Elements of the Java language, from largest to smallest.

The standard edition of Java comes with *several thousand* classes you can import, which can be both exciting and intimidating. You can browse this library at *http://docs.oracle.com/javase/8/docs/api/*. Most of the Java library itself is written in Java.

Note there is a major difference between the Java *language*, which defines the syntax and meaning of the elements in Figure 3-2, and the Java *library*, which provides the built-in classes.

Inches to Centimeters

Now let's see an example that's a little more useful. Although most of the world has adopted the metric system for weights and measures, some countries are stuck with English units. For example, when talking with friends in Europe about the weather, people in the United States might have to convert from Celsius to Fahrenheit and back. Or they might want to convert height in inches to centimeters.

We can write a program to help. We'll use a Scanner to input a measurement in inches, convert to centimeters, and then display the results. The following lines declare the variables and create the Scanner:

```
int inch;
double cm;
Scanner in = new Scanner(System.in);
```

The next step is to prompt the user for the input. We'll use print instead of println so they can enter the input on the same line as the prompt. And we'll use the Scanner method nextInt, which reads input from the keyboard and converts it to an integer:

```
System.out.print("How many inches? ");
inch = in.nextInt();
```

Next we multiply the number of inches by 2.54, since that's how many centimeters there are per inch, and display the results:

```
cm = inch * 2.54;
System.out.print(inch + " in = ");
System.out.println(cm + " cm");
```

This code works correctly, but it has a minor problem. If another programmer reads this code, they might wonder where 2.54 comes from. For the benefit of others (and yourself in the future), it would be better to assign this value to a variable with a meaningful name. We'll demonstrate in the next section.

Literals and Constants

A value that appears in a program, like 2.54 (or " in ="), is called a **literal**. In general, there's nothing wrong with literals. But when numbers like 2.54 appear in an expression with no explanation, they make code hard to read. And if the same value appears many times, and might have to change in the future, it makes code hard to maintain.

Values like that are sometimes called **magic numbers** (with the implication that being "magic" is not a good thing). A good practice is to assign magic numbers to variables with meaningful names, like this:

```
double cmPerInch = 2.54;
cm = inch * cmPerInch;
```

This version is easier to read and less error-prone, but it still has a problem. Variables can vary, but the number of centimeters in an inch does not. Once we assign a value to cmPerInch, it should never change. Java provides a language feature that enforces that rule, the keyword final.

```
final double CM_PER_INCH = 2.54;
```

Declaring that a variable is final means that it cannot be reassigned once it has been initialized. If you try, the compiler reports an error. Variables declared as final are called **constants**. By convention, names for constants are all uppercase, with the underscore character (_) between words.

Formatting Output

When you output a double using print or println, it displays up to 16 decimal places:

```
System.out.print(4.0 / 3.0);
```

The result is:

```
1.3333333333333333
```

That might be more than you want. System.out provides another method, called printf, that gives you more control of the format. The "f" in printf stands for "formatted". Here's an example:

```
System.out.printf("Four thirds = %.3f", 4.0 / 3.0);
```

The first value in the parentheses is a **format string** that specifies how the output should be displayed. This format string contains ordinary text followed by a **format specifier**, which is a special sequence that starts with a percent sign. The format specifier %.3f indicates that the following value should be displayed as floating-point, rounded to three decimal places. The result is:

```
Four thirds = 1.333
```

The format string can contain any number of format specifiers; here's an example with two:

```
int inch = 100;
double cm = inch * CM_PER_INCH;
System.out.printf("%d in = %f cm\n", inch, cm);
```

The result is:

```
100 in = 254.000000 cm
```

Like print, printf does not append a newline. So format strings often end with a newline character.

The format specifier %d displays integer values ("d" stands for "decimal"). The values are matched up with the format specifiers in order, so inch is displayed using %d, and cm is displayed using %f.

Learning about format strings is like learning a sub-language within Java. There are many options, and the details can be overwhelming. Table 3-1 lists a few common uses, to give you an idea of how things work. For more details, refer to the documentation of java.util.Formatter. The easiest way to find documentation for Java classes is to do a web search for "Java" and the name of the class.

Table 3-1. Example format specifiers

%d	decimal integer	12345
%08d	padded with zeros, at least 8 digits wide	00012345
%f	floating-point	6.789000
%.2f	rounded to 2 decimal places	6.79

Centimeters to Inches

Now suppose we have a measurement in centimeters, and we want to round it off to the nearest inch. It is tempting to write:

```
inch = cm / CM_PER_INCH;  // syntax error
```

But the result is an error—you get something like, "Bad types in assignment: from double to int." The problem is that the value on the right is floating-point, and the variable on the left is an integer.

The simplest way to convert a floating-point value to an integer is to use a **type cast**, so called because it molds or "casts" a value from one type to another. The syntax for type casting is to put the name of the type in parentheses and use it as an operator.

```
double pi = 3.14159;
int x = (int) pi;
```

The (int) operator has the effect of converting what follows into an integer. In this example, x gets the value 3. Like integer division, converting to an integer always rounds toward zero, even if the fraction part is 0.999999 (or -0.999999). In other words, it simply throws away the fractional part.

Type casting takes precedence over arithmetic operations. In this example, the value of pi gets converted to an integer before the multiplication. So the result is 60.0, not 62.0.

```
double pi = 3.14159;
double x = (int) pi * 20.0;
```

Keeping that in mind, here's how we can convert a measurement in centimeters to inches:

```
inch = (int) (cm / CM_PER_INCH);
System.out.printf("%f cm = %d in\n", cent, inch);
```

The parentheses after the cast operator require the division to happen before the type cast. And the result is rounded toward zero; we will see in the next chapter how to round floating-point numbers to the closest integer.

Modulus Operator

Let's take the example one step further: suppose you have a measurement in inches and you want to convert to feet and inches. The goal is divide by 12 (the number of inches in a foot) and keep the remainder.

We have already seen the division operator (/), which computes the quotient of two numbers. If the numbers are integers, it performs integer division. Java also provides the **modulus** operator (%), which divides two numbers and computes the remainder.

Using division and modulus, we can convert to feet and inches like this:

```
quotient = 76 / 12;    // division
remainder = 76 % 12;   // modulus
```

The first line yields 6. The second line, which is pronounced "76 mod 12", yields 4. So 76 inches is 6 feet, 4 inches.

The modulus operator looks like a percent sign, but you might find it helpful to think of it as a division sign (÷) rotated to the left.

The modulus operator turns out to be surprisingly useful. For example, you can check whether one number is divisible by another: if x % y is zero, then x is divisible by y. You can use modulus to "extract" digits from a number: x % 10 yields the right-most digit of x, and x % 100 yields the last two digits. Also, many encryption algorithms use the modulus operator extensively.

Putting It All Together

At this point, you have seen enough Java to write useful programs that solve everyday problems. You can (1) import Java library classes, (2) create a Scanner, (3) get input from the keyboard, (4) format output with printf, and (5) divide and mod integers. Now we will put everything together in a complete program:

```java
import java.util.Scanner;

/**
 * Converts centimeters to feet and inches.
 */
public class Convert {

    public static void main(String[] args) {
        double cm;
        int feet, inches, remainder;
        final double CM_PER_INCH = 2.54;
        final int IN_PER_FOOT = 12;
        Scanner in = new Scanner(System.in);

        // prompt the user and get the value
        System.out.print("Exactly how many cm? ");
        cm = in.nextDouble();

        // convert and output the result
        inches = (int) (cm / CM_PER_INCH);
        feet = inches / IN_PER_FOOT;
        remainder = inches % IN_PER_FOOT;
        System.out.printf("%.2f cm = %d ft, %d in\n",
                        cm, feet, remainder);
    }
}
```

Although not required, all variables and constants are declared at the top of main. This practice makes it easier to find their types later on, and it helps the reader know what data is involved in the algorithm.

For readability, each major step of the algorithm is separated by a blank line and begins with a comment. It also includes a documentation comment (/**), which we'll learn more about in the next chapter.

Many algorithms, including the Convert program, perform division and modulus together. In both steps, you divide by the same number (IN_PER_FOOT).

When statements get long (generally wider than 80 characters), a common style convention is to break them across multiple lines. The reader should never have to scroll horizontally.

The Scanner Bug

Now that you've had some experience with Scanner, there is an unexpected behavior we want to warn you about. The following code fragment asks users for their name and age:

```
System.out.print("What is your name? ");
name = in.nextLine();
System.out.print("What is your age? ");
age = in.nextInt();
System.out.printf("Hello %s, age %d\n", name, age);
```

The output might look something like this:

```
Hello Grace Hopper, age 45
```

When you read a String followed by an int, everything works just fine. But when you read an int followed by a String, something strange happens.

```
System.out.print("What is your age? ");
age = in.nextInt();
System.out.print("What is your name? ");
name = in.nextLine();
System.out.printf("Hello %s, age %d\n", name, age);
```

Try running this example code. It doesn't let you input your name, and it immediately displays the output:

```
What is your name? Hello , age 45
```

To understand what is happening, you have to understand that the Scanner doesn't see input as multiple lines, like we do. Instead, it gets a "stream of characters" as shown in Figure 3-3.

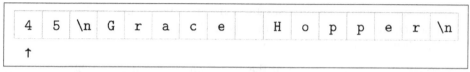

Figure 3-3. A stream of characters as seen by a Scanner.

The arrow indicates the next character to be read by Scanner. When you call nextInt, it reads characters until it gets to a non-digit. Figure 3-4 shows the state of the stream after nextInt is invoked.

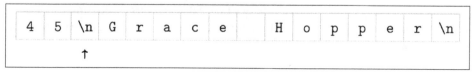

Figure 3-4. A stream of characters after nextInt *is invoked.*

At this point, nextInt returns 45. The program then displays the prompt "What is your name? " and calls nextLine, which reads characters until it gets to a newline. But since the next character is already a newline, nextLine returns the empty string "".

To solve this problem, you need an extra nextLine after nextInt.

```
System.out.print("What is your age? ");
age = in.nextInt();
in.nextLine();  // read the newline
System.out.print("What is your name? ");
name = in.nextLine();
System.out.printf("Hello %s, age %d\n", name, age);
```

This technique is common when reading int or double values that appear on their own line. First you read the number, and then you read the rest of the line, which is just a newline character.

Vocabulary

package:
    A group of classes that are related to each other.

address:
    The location of a value in computer memory, often represented as a hexadecimal integer.

library:
    A collection of packages and classes that are available for use in other programs.

import statement:
> A statement that allows programs to use classes defined in other packages.

token:
> A basic element of a program, such as a word, space, symbol, or number.

literal:
> A value that appears in source code. For example, "Hello" is a string literal and 74 is an integer literal.

magic number:
> A number that appears without explanation as part of an expression. It should generally be replaced with a constant.

constant:
> A variable, declared final, whose value cannot be changed.

format string:
> A string passed to printf to specify the format of the output.

format specifier:
> A special code that begins with a percent sign and specifies the data type and format of the corresponding value.

type cast:
> An operation that explicitly converts one data type into another. In Java it appears as a type name in parentheses, like (int).

modulus:
> An operator that yields the remainder when one integer is divided by another. In Java, it is denoted with a percent sign; for example, 5 % 2 is 1.

Exercises

The code for this chapter is in the ch03 directory of ThinkJavaCode. See "Using the Code Examples" on page xi for instructions on how to download the repository. Before you start the exercises, we recommend that you compile and run the examples.

If you have not already read "Command-Line Interface" on page 203, now might be a good time. It describes the command-line interface, which is a powerful and efficient way to interact with your computer.

Exercise 3-1.

When you use `printf`, the Java compiler does not check your format string. See what happens if you try to display a value with type `int` using `%f`. And what happens if you display a `double` using `%d`? What if you use two format specifiers, but then only provide one value?

Exercise 3-2.

Write a program that converts a temperature from Celsius to Fahrenheit. It should (1) prompt the user for input, (2) read a `double` value from the keyboard, (3) calculate the result, and (4) format the output to one decimal place. For example, it should display `"24.0 C = 75.2 F"`.

Here is the formula. Be careful not to use integer division!

$$F = C \times \frac{9}{5} + 32$$

Exercise 3-3.

Write a program that converts a total number of seconds to hours, minutes, and seconds. It should (1) prompt the user for input, (2) read an integer from the keyboard, (3) calculate the result, and (4) use `printf` to display the output. For example, `"5000 seconds = 1 hours, 23 minutes, and 20 seconds"`.

Hint: Use the modulus operator.

Exercise 3-4.

The goal of this exercise is to program a "Guess My Number" game. When it's finished, it will work like this:

```
I'm thinking of a number between 1 and 100
(including both). Can you guess what it is?
Type a number: 45
Your guess is: 45
The number I was thinking of is: 14
You were off by: 31
```

To choose a random number, you can use the `Random` class in `java.util`. Here's how it works:

```
import java.util.Random;

public class GuessStarter {

    public static void main(String[] args) {
        // pick a random number
        Random random = new Random();
        int number = random.nextInt(100) + 1;
        System.out.println(number);
    }
}
```

Like the Scanner class we saw in this chapter, Random has to be imported before we can use it. And as we saw with Scanner, we have to use the new operator to create a Random (number generator).

Then we can use the method nextInt to generate a random number. In this example, the result of nextInt(100) will be between 0 and 99, including both. Adding 1 yields a number between 1 and 100, including both.

1. The definition of GuessStarter is in a file called GuessStarter.java, in the directory called ch03, in the repository for this book.

2. Compile and run this program.

3. Modify the program to prompt the user, then use a Scanner to read a line of user input. Compile and test the program.

4. Read the user input as an integer and display the result. Again, compile and test.

5. Compute and display the difference between the user's guess and the number that was generated.

CHAPTER 4

Void Methods

So far we've only written short programs that have a single class and a single method (main). In this chapter, we'll show you how to organize longer programs into multiple methods and classes. We'll also present the Math class, which provides methods for common mathematical operations.

Math Methods

In mathematics, you have probably seen functions like sin and log, and you have learned to evaluate expressions like sin ($\pi/2$) and log ($1/x$). First, you evaluate the expression in parentheses, which is called the **argument** of the function. Then you can evaluate the function itself, maybe by punching it into a calculator.

This process can be applied repeatedly to evaluate more complex expressions like log ($1/$ sin ($\pi/2$)). First we evaluate the argument of the innermost function, then evaluate the function itself, and so on.

The Java library includes a Math class that provides common mathematical operations. Math is in the java.lang package, so you don't have to import it. You can use, or **invoke**, Math methods like this:

```
double root = Math.sqrt(17.0);
double angle = 1.5;
double height = Math.sin(angle);
```

The first line sets root to the square root of 17. The third line finds the sine of 1.5 (the value of angle).

Arguments of the trigonometric functions—sin, cos, and tan—should be in *radians*. To convert from degrees to radians, you can divide by 180 and multiply by π. Conveniently, the Math class provides a constant double named PI that contains an approximation of π:

```
double degrees = 90;
double angle = degrees / 180.0 * Math.PI;
```

Notice that PI is in capital letters. Java does not recognize Pi, pi, or pie. Also, PI is the name of a variable, not a method, so it doesn't have parentheses. The same is true for the constant Math.E, which approximates Euler's number.

Converting to and from radians is a common operation, so the Math class provides methods that do it for you.

```
double radians = Math.toRadians(180.0);
double degrees = Math.toDegrees(Math.PI);
```

Another useful method is round, which rounds a floating-point value to the nearest integer and returns a long. A long is like an int, but bigger. More specifically, an int uses 32 bits; the largest value it can hold is $2^{31} - 1$, which is about 2 billion. A long uses 64 bits, so the largest value is $2^{63} - 1$, which is about 9 quintillion.

```
long x = Math.round(Math.PI * 20.0);
```

The result is 63 (rounded up from 62.8319).

Take a minute to read the documentation for these and other methods in the Math class. The easiest way to find documentation for Java classes is to do a web search for "Java" and the name of the class.

Composition Revisited

Just as with mathematical functions, Java methods can be *composed*. That means you can use one expression as part of another. For example, you can use any expression as an argument to a method:

```
double x = Math.cos(angle + Math.PI / 2.0);
```

This statement divides Math.PI by two, adds the result to angle, and computes the cosine of the sum. You can also take the result of one method and pass it as an argument to another:

```
double x = Math.exp(Math.log(10.0));
```

In Java, the log method always uses base e. So this statement finds the log base e of 10, and then raises e to that power. The result gets assigned to x.

Some math methods take more than one argument. For example, Math.pow takes two arguments and raises the first to the power of the second. This line of code assigns the value 1024.0 to the variable x:

```
double x = Math.pow(2.0, 10.0);
```

When using Math methods, it is a common error to forget the Math. For example, if
you try to invoke pow(2.0, 10.0), you get an error message like:

```
File: Test.java  [line: 5]
Error: cannot find symbol
  symbol:   method pow(double,double)
  location: class Test
```

The message "cannot find symbol" is confusing, but the last line provides a useful
hint. The compiler is looking for pow in the same class where it is used, which is Test.
If you don't specify a class name, the compiler looks in the current class.

Adding New Methods

You have probably guessed by now that you can define more than one method in a
class. Here's an example:

```
public class NewLine {

    public static void newLine() {
        System.out.println();
    }

    public static void main(String[] args) {
        System.out.println("First line.");
        newLine();
        System.out.println("Second line.");
    }
}
```

The name of the class is NewLine. By convention, class names begin with a capital letter. NewLine contains two methods, newLine and main. Remember that Java is case-
sensitive, so NewLine and newLine are not the same.

Method names should begin with a lowercase letter and use "camel case", which is a
cute name for jammingWordsTogetherLikeThis. You can use any name you want for
methods, except main or any of the Java keywords.

newLine and main are public, which means they can be invoked from other classes.
They are both static, but we can't explain what that means yet. And they are both
void, which means that they don't yield a result (unlike the Math methods, for example).

The parentheses after the method name contain a list of variables, called **parameters**,
where the method stores its arguments. main has a single parameter, called args,
which has type String[]. That means that whoever invokes main must provide an
array of strings (we'll get to arrays in a later chapter).

Since `newLine` has no parameters, it requires no arguments, as shown when it is invoked in `main`. And because `newLine` is in the same class as `main`, we don't have to specify the class name.

The output of this program is:

```
First line.

Second line.
```

Notice the extra space between the lines. If we wanted more space between them, we could invoke the same method repeatedly:

```
public static void main(String[] args) {
    System.out.println("First line.");
    newLine();
    newLine();
    newLine();
    System.out.println("Second line.");
}
```

Or we could write a new method that displays three blank lines:

```
public static void threeLine() {
    newLine();
    newLine();
    newLine();
}

public static void main(String[] args) {
    System.out.println("First line.");
    threeLine();
    System.out.println("Second line.");
}
```

You can invoke the same method more than once, and you can have one method invoke another. In this example, `main` invokes `threeLine`, and `threeLine` invokes `newLine`.

Beginners often wonder why it is worth the trouble to create new methods. There are many reasons, but this example demonstrates a few of them:

- Creating a new method gives you an opportunity to give a name to a group of statements, which makes code easier to read and understand.
- Introducing new methods can make a program smaller by eliminating repetitive code. For example, to display nine consecutive new lines, you could invoke `threeLine` three times.

- A common problem solving technique is to break tasks down into sub-problems. Methods allow you to focus on each sub-problem in isolation, and then compose them into a complete solution.

Flow of Execution

Pulling together the code from the previous section, the complete program looks like this:

```java
public class NewLine {

    public static void newLine() {
        System.out.println();
    }

    public static void threeLine() {
        newLine();
        newLine();
        newLine();
    }

    public static void main(String[] args) {
        System.out.println("First line.");
        threeLine();
        System.out.println("Second line.");
    }
}
```

When you look at a class definition that contains several methods, it is tempting to read it from top to bottom. But that is likely to be confusing, because that is not the **flow of execution** of the program.

Execution always begins at the first statement of main, regardless of where it is in the source file. Statements are executed one at a time, in order, until you reach a method invocation, which you can think of as a detour. Instead of going to the next statement, you jump to the first line of the invoked method, execute all the statements there, and then come back and pick up exactly where you left off.

That sounds simple enough, but remember that one method can invoke another one. In the middle of main, we go off to execute the statements in threeLine. While we are executing threeLine, we go off to execute newLine. Then newLine invokes println, which causes yet another detour.

Fortunately, Java is good at keeping track of which methods are running. So when println completes, it picks up where it left off in newLine; when newLine completes, it goes back to threeLine, and when threeLine completes, it gets back to main.

In summary, when you read a program, don't read from top to bottom. Instead, follow the flow of execution.

Parameters and Arguments

Some of the methods we have used require arguments, which are the values you provide when you invoke the method. For example, to find the sine of a number, you have to provide the number, so sin takes a double as an argument. To display a message, you have to provide the message, so println takes a String.

When you use a method, you provide the arguments. When you write a method, you name the parameters. The parameter list indicates what arguments are required. The following class shows an example:

```
public class PrintTwice {

    public static void printTwice(String s) {
        System.out.println(s);
        System.out.println(s);
    }

    public static void main(String[] args) {
        printTwice("Don't make me say this twice!");
    }
}
```

printTwice has a parameter named s with type String. When we invoke printTwice, we have to provide an argument with type String.

Before the method executes, the argument gets assigned to the parameter. In this example, the argument "Don't make me say this twice!" gets assigned to the parameter s.

This process is called **parameter passing** because the value gets passed from outside the method to the inside. An argument can be any kind of expression, so if you have a String variable, you can use it as an argument:

```
String argument = "Never say never.";
printTwice(argument);
```

The value you provide as an argument must have the same type as the parameter. For example, if you try:

```
printTwice(17);  // syntax error
```

You will get an error message like this:

```
File: Test.java  [line: 10]
Error: method printTwice in class Test cannot be applied
       to given types;
  required: java.lang.String
  found: int
  reason: actual argument int cannot be converted to
          java.lang.String by method invocation conversion
```

Sometimes Java can convert an argument from one type to another automatically. For example, Math.sqrt requires a double, but if you invoke Math.sqrt(25), the integer value 25 is automatically converted to the floating-point value 25.0. But in the case of printTwice, Java can't (or won't) convert the integer 17 to a String.

Parameters and other variables only exist inside their own methods. Inside main, there is no such thing as s. If you try to use it there, you'll get a compiler error. Similarly, inside printTwice there is no such thing as argument. That variable belongs to main.

Because variables only exist inside the methods where they are defined, they are often called **local variables**.

Multiple Parameters

Here is an example of a method that takes two parameters:

```
public static void printTime(int hour, int minute) {
    System.out.print(hour);
    System.out.print(":");
    System.out.println(minute);
}
```

In the parameter list, it may be tempting to write:

```
public static void printTime(int hour, minute) {
    ...
```

But that format (without the second int) is only legal for variable declarations. In parameter lists, you need to specify the type of each variable separately.

To invoke this method, we have to provide two integers as arguments:

```
int hour = 11;
int minute = 59;
printTime(hour, minute);
```

A common error is to declare the types of the arguments, like this:

```
int hour = 11;
int minute = 59;
printTime(int hour, int minute);  // syntax error
```

That's a syntax error; the compiler sees `int hour` and `int minute` as variable declarations, not expressions. You wouldn't declare the types of the arguments if they were simply integers:

```
printTime(int 11, int 59);  // syntax error
```

Stack Diagrams

Pulling together the code fragments from the previous section, here is a complete class definition:

```
public class PrintTime {

    public static void printTime(int hour, int minute) {
        System.out.print(hour);
        System.out.print(":");
        System.out.println(minute);
    }

    public static void main(String[] args) {
        int hour = 11;
        int minute = 59;
        printTime(hour, minute);
    }
}
```

`printTime` has two parameters, named `hour` and `minute`. And `main` has two variables, also named `hour` and `minute`. Although they have the same names, these variables are not the same. `hour` in `printTime` and `hour` in `main` refer to different storage locations, and they can have different values.

For example, you could invoke `printTime` like this:

```
int hour = 11;
int minute = 59;
printTime(hour + 1, 0);
```

Before the method is invoked, Java evaluates the arguments; in this example, the results are 12 and 0. Then it assigns those values to the parameters. Inside `printTime`, the value of `hour` is 12, not 11, and the value of `minute` is 0, not 59. Furthermore, if `printTime` modifies one of its parameters, that change has no effect on the variables in `main`.

One way to keep track of everything is to draw a **stack diagram**, which is a state diagram (see "State Diagrams" on page 15) that shows method invocations. For each method there is a box called a **frame** that contains the method's parameters and variables. The name of the method appears outside the frame; the variables and parameters appear inside.

As with state diagrams, stack diagrams show variables and methods at a particular point in time. Figure 4-1 is a stack diagram at the beginning of the printTime method.

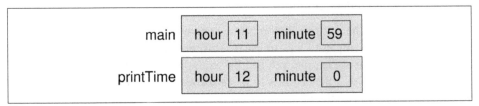

Figure 4-1. Stack diagram for PrintTime.

Reading Documentation

One of the nice things about Java is that it comes with an extensive library of classes and methods. But before you use them, you might have to read the documentation. And sometimes that's not easy.

As an example, let's look at the documentation for Scanner, which we used in "The Scanner Class" on page 30. You can find it by doing a web search for "Java Scanner". Figure 4-2 shows a screenshot of the page.

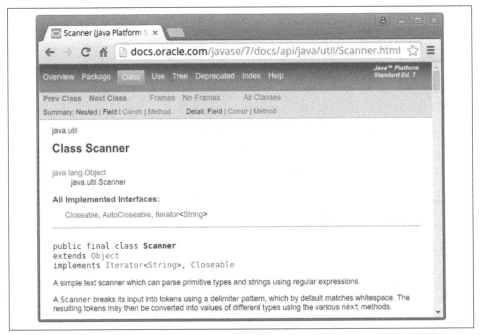

Figure 4-2. Screenshot of the documentation for Scanner.

Documentation for other classes uses a similar format. The first line is the package that contains the class, such as `java.util`. The second line is the name of the class. The "Implemented Interfaces" section lists some of the things a `Scanner` can do; we won't say more about that for now.

The next section of the documentation is a narrative that explains the purpose of the class and includes examples of how to use it. This text can be difficult to read because it uses terms we have not learned yet. But the examples are often very useful. A good way to get started with a new class is to paste the examples into a test file and see if you can compile and run them.

One of the examples shows how you can use a `Scanner` to read input from a `String` instead of `System.in`:

```
String input = "1 fish 2 fish red fish blue fish";
Scanner s = new Scanner(input);
```

After the narrative, code examples, and some other details, you will find the following tables:

Constructor summary:
Ways of creating, or "constructing", a `Scanner`.

Method summary:
The list of methods that `Scanner` provides.

Constructor detail:
More information about how to create a `Scanner`.

Method detail:
More information about each method.

As an example, here is the summary information for `nextInt`:

```
public int nextInt()
Scans the next token of the input as an int.
```

The first line is the method's **signature**, which specifies the name of the method, its parameters (none), and what type it returns (`int`). The next line is a short description of what it does.

The "Method detail" explains more:

```
public int nextInt()
Scans the next token of the input as an int.

An invocation of this method of the form nextInt() behaves in
exactly the same way as the invocation nextInt(radix), where
radix is the default radix of this scanner.

Returns:
the int scanned from the input
```

```
Throws:
InputMismatchException - if the next token does not match
    the Integer regular expression, or is out of range
NoSuchElementException - if input is exhausted
IllegalStateException - if this scanner is closed
```

The "Returns" section describes the result when the method succeeds. In contrast, the "Throws" section describes possible errors and their resulting exceptions. Exceptions are said to be "thrown", like a referee throwing a flag, or like a toddler throwing a fit.

It might take you some time to get comfortable reading documentation and learning which parts to ignore. But it's worth the effort. Knowing what's available in the library helps you avoid reinventing the wheel. And a little bit of documentation can save you a lot of debugging.

Writing Documentation

As you benefit from reading good documentation, you should "pay it forward" by writing good documentation. A nice feature of the Java language is the ability to embed documentation in your source code. That way, you can write it as you go, and as things change, it is easier to keep the documentation consistent with the code.

If you include documentation in your source code, you can extract it automatically, and generate well-formatted HTML, using a tool called **Javadoc**. This tool is included in standard Java development environments, and it is widely used. In fact, the online documentation of the Java libraries is generated by Javadoc.

Javadoc scans your source files looking for specially-formatted **documentation comments,** also known as "Javadoc comments". They begin with /** (two stars) and end with */ (one star). Anything in between is considered part of the documentation.

Here's a class definition with two Javadoc comments, one for the class and one for the main method:

```
/**
 * Example program that demonstrates print vs println.
 */
public class Goodbye {

    /**
     * Prints a greeting.
     */
    public static void main(String[] args) {
        System.out.print("Goodbye, ");  // note the space
        System.out.println("cruel world");
    }
}
```

The class comment explains the purpose of the class. The method comment explains what the method does.

Notice that this example also includes an inline comment, beginning with //. In general, inline comments are short phrases that help explain complex parts of a program. They are intended for other programmers reading and maintaining the source code.

In contrast, Javadoc comments are longer, usually complete sentences. They explain what each method does, but they omit details about how the method works. And they are intended for people who will use the methods without looking at the source code.

Appropriate comments and documentation are essential for making source code readable. And remember that the person most likely to read your code in the future, and appreciate good documentation, is you.

Vocabulary

argument:
> A value that you provide when you invoke a method. This value must have the same type as the corresponding parameter.

invoke:
> To cause a method to execute. Also known as "calling" a method.

parameter:
> A piece of information that a method requires before it can run. Parameters are variables: they contain values and have types.

flow of execution:
> The order in which Java executes methods and statements. It may not necessarily be from top to bottom, left to right.

parameter passing:
> The process of assigning an argument value to a parameter variable.

local variable:
> A variable declared inside a method. Local variables cannot be accessed from outside their method.

stack diagram:
> A graphical representation of the variables belonging to each method. The method calls are "stacked" from top to bottom, in the flow of execution.

frame:
> In a stack diagram, a representation of the variables and parameters for a method, along with their current values.

signature:
> The first line of a method that defines its name, return type, and parameters.

Javadoc:
> A tool that reads Java source code and generates documentation in HTML format.

documentation:
> Comments that describe the technical operation of a class or method.

Exercises

The code for this chapter is in the ch04 directory of ThinkJavaCode. See "Using the Code Examples" on page xi for instructions on how to download the repository. Before you start the exercises, we recommend that you compile and run the examples.

If you have not already read "Command-Line Testing" on page 204, now might be a good time. It describes an efficient way to test programs that take input from the user and display specific output.

Exercise 4-1.

The point of this exercise is to practice reading code and to make sure that you understand the flow of execution through a program with multiple methods.

1. What is the output of the following program? Be precise about where there are spaces and where there are newlines.

   Hint: Start by describing in words what ping and baffle do when they are invoked.

2. Draw a stack diagram that shows the state of the program the first time ping is invoked.

3. What happens if you invoke baffle(); at the end of the ping method? (We will see why in the next chapter.)

```java
public static void zoop() {
    baffle();
    System.out.print("You wugga ");
    baffle();
}

public static void main(String[] args) {
    System.out.print("No, I ");
    zoop();
    System.out.print("I ");
    baffle();
}
```

```
public static void baffle() {
    System.out.print("wug");
    ping();
}

public static void ping() {
    System.out.println(".");
}
```

Exercise 4-2.

The point of this exercise is to make sure you understand how to write and invoke methods that take parameters.

1. Write the first line of a method named `zool` that takes three parameters: an `int` and two `String`s.

2. Write a line of code that calls `zool`, passing as arguments the value `11`, the name of your first pet, and the name of the street you grew up on.

Exercise 4-3.

The purpose of this exercise is to take code from a previous exercise and encapsulate it in a method that takes parameters. You should start with a working solution to Exercise 2-2.

1. Write a method called `printAmerican` that takes the day, date, month and year as parameters and that displays them in American format.

2. Test your method by invoking it from `main` and passing appropriate arguments. The output should look something like this (except that the date might be different):

   `Saturday, July 22, 2015`

3. Once you have debugged `printAmerican`, write another method called `printEuropean` that displays the date in European format.

CHAPTER 5

Conditionals and Logic

The programs we've seen in previous chapters do pretty much the same thing every time, regardless of the input. For more complex computations, programs usually react to the inputs, check for certain conditions, and generate appropriate results. This chapter presents the features you need for programs to make decisions: a new data type called `boolean`, operators for expressing logic, and `if` statements.

Relational Operators

Relational operators are used to check conditions like whether two values are equal, or whether one is greater than the other. The following expressions show how they are used:

```
x == y      // x is equal to y
x != y      // x is not equal to y
x > y       // x is greater than y
x < y       // x is less than y
x >= y      // x is greater than or equal to y
x <= y      // x is less than or equal to y
```

The result of a relational operator is one of two special values, `true` or `false`. These values belong to the data type `boolean`; in fact, they are the only boolean values.

You are probably familiar with these operations, but notice that the Java operators are different from the mathematical symbols like =, ≠, and ≤. A common error is to use a single = instead of a double ==. Remember that = is the assignment operator, and == is a comparison operator. Also, there is no such thing as the =< or => operators.

The two sides of a relational operator have to be compatible. For example, the expression 5 < "6" is invalid because 5 is an `int` and "6" is a `String`. When comparing values of different numeric types, Java applies the same conversion rules we saw previously with the assignment operator. For example, when evaluating the expression 5 < 6.0, Java automatically converts the 5 to 5.0.

Most relational operators don't work with strings. But confusingly, == and != do work with strings—they just don't do what you expect. We'll explain what they do later; in the meantime, don't use them with strings. Instead, you should use the equals method:

```java
String fruit1 = "Apple";
String fruit2 = "Orange";
System.out.println(fruit1.equals(fruit2));
```

The result of fruit1.equals(fruit2) is the boolean value false.

Logical Operators

Java has three **logical operators**: &&, ||, and !, which respectively stand for *and, or,* and *not*. The results of these operators are similar to their meanings in English.

For example, x > 0 && x < 10 is true when x is both greater than zero *and* less than 10. The expression evenFlag || n % 3 == 0 is true if either condition is true, that is, if evenFlag is true *or* the number n is divisible by 3. Finally, the ! operator inverts a boolean expression. So !evenFlag is true if evenFlag is *not* true.

Logical operators evaluate the second expression only when necessary. For example, true || anything is always true, so Java does not need to evaluate the expression anything. Likewise, false && anything is always false. Ignoring the second operand, when possible, is called **short circuit** evaluation, by analogy with an electrical circuit. Short circuit evaluation can save time, especially if anything takes a long time to evaluate. It can also avoid unnecessary errors, if anything might fail.

If you ever have to negate an expression that contains logical operators, and you probably will, **De Morgan's laws** can help:

- !(A && B) is the same as !A || !B
- !(A || B) is the same as !A && !B

Negating a logical expression is the same as negating each term and changing the operator. The ! operator takes precedence over && and ||, so you don't have to put parentheses around the individual terms !A and !B.

De Morgan's laws also apply to the relational operators. In this case, negating each term means using the "opposite" relational operator.

- `!(x < 5 && y == 3)` is the same as `x >= 5 || y != 3`
- `!(x >= 1 || y != 7)` is the same as `x < 1 && y == 7`

It may help to read these examples out loud in English. For instance, "If I don't want the case where x is less than 5 and y is 3, then I need x to be greater than or equal to 5, or I need y to be anything but 3."

Conditional Statements

To write useful programs, we almost always need to check conditions and react accordingly. **Conditional statements** give us this ability. The simplest conditional statement in Java is the `if` statement:

```
if (x > 0) {
    System.out.println("x is positive");
}
```

The expression in parentheses is called the condition. If it is true, the statements in braces get executed. If the condition is false, execution skips over that block of code. The condition in parentheses can be any boolean expression.

A second form of conditional statement has two possibilities, indicated by `if` and `else`. The possibilities are called **branches**, and the condition determines which one gets executed:

```
if (x % 2 == 0) {
    System.out.println("x is even");
} else {
    System.out.println("x is odd");
}
```

If the remainder when x is divided by 2 is zero, we know that x is even, and this fragment displays a message to that effect. If the condition is false, the second print statement is executed instead. Since the condition must be true or false, exactly one of the branches will run.

The braces are optional for branches that have only one statement. So we could have written the previous example this way:

```
if (x % 2 == 0)
    System.out.println("x is even");
else
    System.out.println("x is odd");
```

However, it's better to use braces—even when they are optional—to avoid making the mistake of adding statements to an `if` or `else` block and forgetting to add the braces.

```
if (x > 0)
    System.out.println("x is positive");
    System.out.println("x is not zero");
```

This code is misleading because it's not indented correctly. Since there are no braces, only the first `println` is part of the `if` statement. Here is what the compiler actually sees:

```
if (x > 0) {
    System.out.println("x is positive");
}
    System.out.println("x is not zero");
```

As a result, the second `println` runs no matter what. Even experienced programmers make this mistake; search the web for Apple's "goto fail" bug.

Chaining and Nesting

Sometimes you want to check related conditions and choose one of several actions. One way to do this is by **chaining** a series of `if` and `else` statements:

```
if (x > 0) {
    System.out.println("x is positive");
} else if (x < 0) {
    System.out.println("x is negative");
} else {
    System.out.println("x is zero");
}
```

These chains can be as long as you want, although they can be difficult to read if they get out of hand. One way to make them easier to read is to use standard indentation, as demonstrated in these examples. If you keep all the statements and braces lined up, you are less likely to make syntax errors.

In addition to chaining, you can also make complex decisions by **nesting** one conditional statement inside another. We could have written the previous example as:

```
if (x == 0) {
    System.out.println("x is zero");
} else {
    if (x > 0) {
        System.out.println("x is positive");
    } else {
        System.out.println("x is negative");
    }
}
```

The outer conditional has two branches. The first branch contains a `print` statement, and the second branch contains another conditional statement, which has two branches of its own. These two branches are also `print` statements, but they could have been conditional statements as well.

These kinds of nested structures are common, but they get difficult to read very quickly. Good indentation is essential to make the structure (or intended structure) apparent to the reader.

Flag Variables

To store a `true` or `false` value, you need a `boolean` variable. You can create one like this:

```
boolean flag;
flag = true;
boolean testResult = false;
```

The first line is a variable declaration, the second is an assignment, and the third is both. Since relational operators evaluate to a `boolean` value, you can store the result of a comparison in a variable:

```
boolean evenFlag = (n % 2 == 0);     // true if n is even
boolean positiveFlag = (x > 0);      // true if x is positive
```

The parentheses are unnecessary, but they make the code easier to read. A variable defined in this way is called a **flag**, because it signals or "flags" the presence or absence of a condition.

You can use flag variables as part of a conditional statement later:

```
if (evenFlag) {
    System.out.println("n was even when I checked it");
}
```

Notice that you don't have to write `if (evenFlag == true)`. Since `evenFlag` is a `boolean`, it's already a condition. Likewise, to check if a flag is `false`:

```
if (!evenFlag) {
    System.out.println("n was odd when I checked it");
}
```

The return Statement

The `return` statement allows you to terminate a method before you reach the end of it. One reason to use `return` is if you detect an error condition:

```
public static void printLogarithm(double x) {
    if (x <= 0.0) {
        System.err.println("Error: x must be positive.");
        return;
    }
    double result = Math.log(x);
    System.out.println("The log of x is " + result);
}
```

This example defines a method named `printLogarithm` that takes a `double` value (named x) as a parameter. It checks whether x is less than or equal to zero, in which case it displays an error message and then uses `return` to exit the method. The flow of execution immediately returns to where the method was invoked, and the remaining lines of the method are not executed.

This example uses `System.err`, which is an `OutputStream` normally used for error messages and warnings. Some development environments display output to `System.err` with a different color or in a separate window.

Validating Input

Here is a method that uses `printLogarithm` from the previous section:

```
public static void scanDouble(Scanner in) {
    System.out.print("Enter a number: ");
    double x = in.nextDouble();
    printLogarithm(x);
}
```

This example uses `nextDouble`, so the `Scanner` (provided by the main method) tries to read a `double`. If the user enters a floating-point number, the `Scanner` converts it to a `double`. But if the user types anything else, the `Scanner` throws an `InputMismatchException`.

We can prevent this error by checking the input before parsing it:

```
public static void scanDouble(Scanner in) {
    System.out.print("Enter a number: ");
    if (!in.hasNextDouble()) {
        String word = in.next();
        System.err.println(word + " is not a number");
        return;
    }
    double x = in.nextDouble();
    printLogarithm(x);
}
```

The `Scanner` class provides `hasNextDouble`, which checks whether the next token in the input stream can be interpreted as a `double`. If so, we can call `nextDouble` with no chance of throwing an exception. If not, we display an error message and return.

Recursive Methods

Now that we have conditional statements, we can explore one of the most magical things a program can do: **recursion**. Consider the following example:

```
public static void countdown(int n) {
    if (n == 0) {
        System.out.println("Blastoff!");
    } else {
        System.out.println(n);
        countdown(n - 1);
    }
}
```

The name of the method is countdown; it takes a single integer as a parameter. If the parameter is zero, it displays the word "Blastoff". Otherwise, it displays the number and then invokes *itself*, passing n - 1 as the argument. A method that invokes itself is called **recursive**.

What happens if we invoke countdown(3) from main?

The execution of countdown begins with n == 3, and since n is not zero, it displays the value 3, and then invokes itself...

The execution of countdown begins with n == 2, and since n is not zero, it displays the value 2, and then invokes itself...

The execution of countdown begins with n == 1, and since n is not zero, it displays the value 1, and then invokes itself...

The execution of countdown begins with n == 0, and since n is zero, it displays the word "Blastoff!" and then returns.

The countdown that got n == 1 returns.

The countdown that got n == 2 returns.

The countdown that got n == 3 returns.

And then you're back in main. So the total output looks like:

```
3
2
1
Blastoff!
```

As a second example, we'll rewrite the methods newLine and threeLine from "Adding New Methods" on page 45.

```
public static void newLine() {
    System.out.println();
}

public static void threeLine() {
    newLine();
    newLine();
    newLine();
}
```

Although these methods work, they would not help if we wanted to display two new-lines, or maybe 100. A better alternative would be:

```
public static void nLines(int n) {
    if (n > 0) {
        System.out.println();
        nLines(n - 1);
    }
}
```

This method takes an integer, n, as a parameter and displays n newlines. The structure is similar to countdown. As long as *n* is greater than zero, it displays a newline and then invokes itself to display (*n* − 1) additional newlines. The total number of new-lines is 1 + (*n* − 1), which is just what we wanted: *n*.

Recursive Stack Diagrams

In the previous chapter, we used a stack diagram to represent the state of a program during a method invocation. The same kind of diagram can make it easier to interpret a recursive method.

Remember that every time a method gets called, Java creates a new frame that contains the current method's parameters and variables. Figure 5-1 is a stack diagram for countdown, called with n == 3.

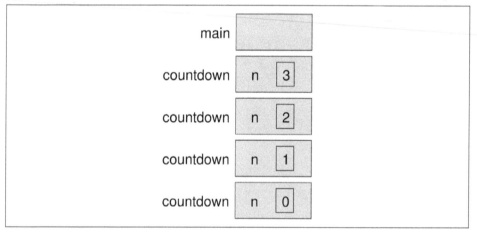

Figure 5-1. Stack diagram for the countdown program.

By convention, the stack for main is at the top and the stack grows down. The frame for main is empty because main does not have any variables. (It has the parameter args, but since we're not using it, we left it out of the diagram.)

There are four frames for countdown, each with a different value for the parameter n. The last frame, with n == 0, is called the **base case**. It does not make a recursive call, so there are no more frames below it.

If there is no base case in a recursive method, or if the base case is never reached, the stack would grow forever, at least in theory. In practice, the size of the stack is limited; if you exceed the limit, you get a StackOverflowError.

For example, here is a recursive method without a base case:

```java
public static void forever(String s) {
    System.out.println(s);
    forever(s);
}
```

This method displays the string until the stack overflows, at which point it throws an exception.

Binary Numbers

The countdown example has three parts: (1) it checks the base case, (2) displays something, and (3) makes a recursive call. What do you think happens if you reverse steps 2 and 3, making the recursive call *before* displaying?

```java
public static void countup(int n) {
    if (n == 0) {
        System.out.println("Blastoff!");
    } else {
        countup(n - 1);
        System.out.println(n);
    }
}
```

The stack diagram is the same as before, and the method is still called *n* times. But now the System.out.println happens just before each recursive call returns. As a result, it counts up instead of down:

```
Blastoff!
1
2
3
```

This behavior comes in handy when it is easier to compute results in reverse order. For example, to convert a decimal integer into its **binary** representation, you repeatedly divide the number by two:

```
23 / 2 is 11 remainder 1
11 / 2 is  5 remainder 1
 5 / 2 is  2 remainder 1
 2 / 2 is  1 remainder 0
 1 / 2 is  0 remainder 1
```

Reading these remainders from bottom to top, 23 in binary is 10111. For more background about binary numbers, see *http://www.mathsisfun.com/binary-number-system.html*.

Here is a recursive method that displays the binary representation of any positive integer:

```java
public static void displayBinary(int value) {
    if (value > 0) {
        displayBinary(value / 2);
        System.out.print(value % 2);
    }
}
```

If `value` is zero, `displayBinary` does nothing (that's the base case). If the argument is positive, the method divides it by two and calls `displayBinary` recursively. When the recursive call returns, the method displays one digit of the result and returns (again).

The leftmost digit is at the bottom of the stack, so it gets displayed first. The rightmost digit, at the top of the stack, gets displayed last. After invoking `displayBinary`, we use `println` to complete the output.

```java
displayBinary(23);
System.out.println();
// output is 10111
```

Learning to think recursively is an important aspect of learning to think like a computer scientist. Many algorithms can be written concisely with recursive methods that perform computations on the way down, on the way up, or both.

Vocabulary

boolean:
> A data type with only two values, `true` and `false`.

relational operator:
> An operator that compares two values and produces a `boolean` indicating the relationship between them.

logical operator:
> An operator that combines boolean values and produces a boolean value.

short circuit:
> A way of evaluating logical operators that only evaluates the second operand if necessary.

De Morgan's laws:
> Mathematical rules that show how to negate a logical expression.

conditional statement:
> A statement that uses a condition to determine which statements to execute.

branch:
> One of the alternative sets of statements inside a conditional statement.

chaining:
> A way of joining several conditional statements in sequence.

nesting:
> Putting a conditional statement inside one or both branches of another conditional statement.

flag:
> A variable (usually `boolean`) that represents a condition or status.

recursion:
> The process of invoking (and restarting) the same method that is currently executing.

recursive:
> A method that invokes itself, usually with different arguments.

base case:
> A condition that causes a recursive method *not* to make another recursive call.

binary:
> A system that uses only zeros and ones to represent numbers. Also known as "base 2".

Exercises

The code for this chapter is in the `ch05` directory of `ThinkJavaCode`. See "Using the Code Examples" on page xi for instructions on how to download the repository. Before you start the exercises, we recommend that you compile and run the examples.

If you have not already read "Tracing with a Debugger" on page 207, now might be a good time. It describes the DrJava debugger, which is a useful tool for tracing the flow of execution.

Exercise 5-1.

Logical operators can simplify nested conditional statements. For example, can you rewrite this code using a single `if` statement?

```
if (x > 0) {
    if (x < 10) {
        System.out.println("positive single digit number.");
    }
}
```

Exercise 5-2.

For the following program:

1. Draw a stack diagram that shows the state of the program the *second* time zoop is invoked.

2. What is the complete output?

```
public static void zoop(String fred, int bob) {
    System.out.println(fred);
    if (bob == 5) {
        ping("not ");
    } else {
        System.out.println("!");
    }
}

public static void main(String[] args) {
    int bizz = 5;
    int buzz = 2;
    zoop("just for", bizz);
    clink(2 * buzz);
}

public static void clink(int fork) {
    System.out.print("It's ");
    zoop("breakfast ", fork);
}

public static void ping(String strangStrung) {
    System.out.println("any " + strangStrung + "more ");
}
```

Exercise 5-3.

Draw a stack diagram that shows the state of the program in "Recursive Methods" on page 62 after main invokes nLines with the parameter n == 4, just before the last invocation of nLines returns.

Exercise 5-4.

Fermat's Last Theorem says that there are no integers a, b, and c such that $a^n + b^n = c^n$, except when $n \leq 2$.

Write a method named checkFermat that takes four integers as parameters—a, b, c and n—and checks to see if Fermat's theorem holds. If n is greater than 2 and $a^n + b^n = c^n$, the program should display "Holy smokes, Fermat was wrong!" Otherwise the program should display "No, that doesn't work."

Hint: You may want to use Math.pow.

Exercise 5-5.

The purpose of this exercise is to take a problem and break it into smaller problems, and to solve the smaller problems by writing simple methods. Consider the first verse of the song "99 Bottles of Beer":

> 99 bottles of beer on the wall,
> 99 bottles of beer,
> ya' take one down, ya' pass it around,
> 98 bottles of beer on the wall.

Subsequent verses are identical except that the number of bottles gets smaller by one in each verse, until the last verse:

> No bottles of beer on the wall,
> no bottles of beer,
> ya' can't take one down, ya' can't pass it around,
> 'cause there are no more bottles of beer on the wall!

And then the song (finally) ends.

Write a program that displays the entire lyrics of "99 Bottles of Beer". Your program should include a recursive method that does the hard part, but you might want to write additional methods to separate other parts of the program. As you develop your code, test it with a small number of verses, like 3.

Exercise 5-6.

This exercise reviews the flow of execution through a program with multiple methods. Read the following code and answer the questions.

```
public class Buzz {

    public static void baffle(String blimp) {
        System.out.println(blimp);
        zippo("ping", -5);
    }

    public static void zippo(String quince, int flag) {
        if (flag < 0) {
            System.out.println(quince + " zoop");
        } else {
            System.out.println("ik");
            baffle(quince);
            System.out.println("boo-wa-ha-ha");
        }
    }

    public static void main(String[] args) {
        zippo("rattle", 13);
    }

}
```

1. Write the number 1 next to the first line of code in this program that will execute.

2. Write the number 2 next to the second line of code, and so on until the end of the program. If a line is executed more than once, it might end up with more than one number next to it.

3. What is the value of the parameter blimp when baffle gets invoked?

4. What is the output of this program?

Exercise 5-7.

Now that we have conditional statements, we can get back to the "Guess My Number" game from Exercise 3-4.

You should already have a program that chooses a random number, prompts the user to guess it, and displays the difference between the guess and the chosen number.

Adding a small amount of code at a time, and testing as you go, modify the program so it tells the user whether the guess is too high or too low, and then prompts the user for another guess.

The program should continue until the user gets it right. *Hint:* Use two methods, and make one of them recursive.

CHAPTER 6

Value Methods

Some of the methods we have used, like the Math methods, return values. But all the methods we have *written* so far have been void; that is, they don't return values. In this chapter, we'll write methods that return values, which we call **value methods**.

Return Values

When you invoke a void method, the invocation is usually on a line all by itself. For example, here is the countup method from "Recursive Methods" on page 62:

```java
public static void countup(int n) {
    if (n == 0) {
        System.out.println("Blastoff!");
    } else {
        countup(n - 1);
        System.out.println(n);
    }
}
```

And here is how it is invoked:

```java
countup(3);
System.out.println("Have a nice day.");
```

On the other hand, when you invoke a value method, you have to do something with the return value. We usually assign it to a variable or use it as part of an expression, like this:

```java
double error = Math.abs(expected - actual);
double height = radius * Math.sin(angle);
```

Compared to void methods, value methods differ in two ways:

- They declare the type of the return value (the **return type**);
- They use at least one return statement to provide a **return value**.

Here's an example: calculateArea takes a double as a parameter and returns the area of a circle with that radius:

```
public static double calculateArea(double radius) {
    double result = Math.PI * radius * radius;
    return result;
}
```

As usual, this method is public and static. But in the place where we are used to seeing void, we see double, which means that the return value from this method is a double.

The last line is a new form of the return statement that includes a return value. This statement means, "return immediately from this method and use the following expression as the return value." The expression you provide can be arbitrarily complex, so we could have written this method more concisely:

```
public static double calculateArea(double radius) {
    return Math.PI * radius * radius;
}
```

On the other hand, **temporary variables** like result often make debugging easier, especially when you are stepping through code using an interactive debugger (see "Tracing with a Debugger" on page 207).

The type of the expression in the return statement must match the return type of the method. When you declare that the return type is double, you are making a promise that this method will eventually produce a double value. If you try to return with no expression, or an expression with the wrong type, the compiler will generate an error.

Sometimes it is useful to have multiple return statements, for example, one in each branch of a conditional:

```
public static double absoluteValue(double x) {
    if (x < 0) {
        return -x;
    } else {
        return x;
    }
}
```

Since these return statements are in a conditional statement, only one will be executed. As soon as either of them executes, the method terminates without executing any more statements.

Code that appears after a `return` statement (in the same block), or any place else where it can never be executed, is called **dead code**. The compiler will give you an "unreachable statement" error if part of your code is dead. For example, this method contains dead code:

```
public static double absoluteValue(double x) {
    if (x < 0) {
        return -x;
    } else {
        return x;
    }
    System.out.println("This line is dead.");
}
```

If you put `return` statements inside a conditional statement, you have to make sure that *every possible path* through the program reaches a `return` statement. The compiler will let you know if that's not the case. For example, the following method is incomplete:

```
public static double absoluteValue(double x) {
    if (x < 0) {
        return -x;
    } else if (x > 0) {
        return x;
    }
    // syntax error
}
```

When x is 0, neither condition is true, so the method ends without hitting a return statement. The error message in this case might be something like "missing return statement", which is confusing since there are already two of them. But hopefully you will know what it means.

Writing Methods

Beginners often make the mistake of writing a lot of code before they try to compile and run it. Then they spend way too much time debugging. A better approach is what we call **incremental development**. The key aspects of incremental development are:

- Start with a working program and make small, incremental changes. At any point, if there is an error, you will know where to look.
- Use variables to hold intermediate values so you can check them, either with print statements or by using a debugger.
- Once the program is working, you can consolidate multiple statements into compound expressions (but only if it does not make the program more difficult to read).

As an example, suppose you want to find the distance between two points, given by the coordinates (x_1, y_1) and (x_2, y_2). By the usual definition:

$$distance = \sqrt{(x_2 - x_1)^2 + (y_2 - y_1)^2}$$

The first step is to consider what a distance method should look like in Java. In other words, what are the inputs (parameters) and what is the output (return value)? In this case, the two points are the parameters, and it is natural to represent them using four double values. The return value is the distance, which should also have type double.

Already we can write an outline for the method, which is sometimes called a **stub**. The stub includes the method signature and a return statement:

```java
public static double distance
        (double x1, double y1, double x2, double y2) {
    return 0.0;
}
```

The return statement is a placeholder that is necessary for the program to compile. At this stage the program doesn't do anything useful, but it is good to compile it so we can find any syntax errors before we add more code.

It's usually a good idea to think about testing *before* you develop new methods; doing so can help you figure out how to implement them. To test the method, we can invoke it from main using sample values:

```java
double dist = distance(1.0, 2.0, 4.0, 6.0);
```

With these values, the horizontal distance is 3.0 and the vertical distance is 4.0. So the result should be 5.0, the hypotenuse of a 3-4-5 triangle. When you are testing a method, it is helpful to know the right answer.

Once we have compiled the stub, we can start adding lines of code one at a time. After each incremental change, we recompile and run the program. If there is an error at any point, we have a good idea where to look: the last line we added.

The next step is to find the differences $x_2 - x_1$ and $y_2 - y_1$. We store those values in temporary variables named dx and dy.

```java
public static double distance
        (double x1, double y1, double x2, double y2) {
    double dx = x2 - x1;
    double dy = y2 - y1;
    System.out.println("dx is " + dx);
    System.out.println("dy is " + dy);
    return 0.0;
}
```

The print statements allows us to check the intermediate values before proceeding. They should be 3.0 and 4.0. We will remove the print statements when the method is finished. Code like that is called **scaffolding**, because it is helpful for building the program, but it is not part of the final product.

The next step is to square dx and dy. We could use the Math.pow method, but it is simpler to multiply each term by itself.

```
public static double distance
        (double x1, double y1, double x2, double y2) {
    double dx = x2 - x1;
    double dy = y2 - y1;
    double dsquared = dx * dx + dy * dy;
    System.out.println("dsquared is " + dsquared);
    return 0.0;
}
```

Again, you should compile and run the program at this stage and check the intermediate value, which should be 25.0. Finally, we can use Math.sqrt to compute and return the result.

```
public static double distance
        (double x1, double y1, double x2, double y2) {
    double dx = x2 - x1;
    double dy = y2 - y1;
    double dsquared = dx * dx + dy * dy;
    double result = Math.sqrt(dsquared);
    return result;
}
```

As you gain more experience programming, you might write and debug more than one line at a time. Nevertheless, incremental development can save you a lot of time.

Method Composition

Once you define a new method, you can use it as part of an expression, or build new methods using existing methods. For example, suppose someone gave you two points, the center of the circle and a point on the perimeter, and asked for the area of the circle. Let's say the center point is stored in the variables xc and yc, and the perimeter point is in xp and yp.

The first step is to find the radius of the circle, which is the distance between the two points. Fortunately, we have a method that does just that (distance).

```
double radius = distance(xc, yc, xp, yp);
```

The second step is to find the area of a circle with that radius. We have a method for that computation too (calculateArea).

```
        double area = calculateArea(radius);
        return area;
```

Putting everything together in a new method, we get:

```
public static double circleArea
        (double xc, double yc, double xp, double yp) {
    double radius = distance(xc, yc, xp, yp);
    double area = calculateArea(radius);
    return area;
}
```

The temporary variables `radius` and `area` are useful for development and debugging, but once the program is working we can make it more concise by composing the method calls:

```
public static double circleArea
        (double xc, double yc, double xp, double yp) {
    return calculateArea(distance(xc, yc, xp, yp));
}
```

This example demonstrates a process called **functional decomposition**; that is, breaking a complex computation into simple methods, testing the methods in isolation, and then composing the methods to perform the computation. This process reduces debugging time and yields code that is more likely to be correct and easier to maintain.

Overloading

You might have noticed that `circleArea` and `calculateArea` perform similar functions. They both find the area of a circle, but they take different parameters. For `calculateArea`, we have to provide the radius; for `circleArea` we provide two points.

If two methods do the same thing, it is natural to give them the same name. Having more than one method with the same name is called **overloading**, and it is legal in Java as long as each version takes different parameters. So we could rename `circleArea` to `calculateArea`:

```
public static double calculateArea
        (double xc, double yc, double xp, double yp) {
    return calculateArea(distance(xc, yc, xp, yp));
}
```

Note that this new `calculateArea` method is *not* recursive. When you invoke an overloaded method, Java knows which version you want by looking at the arguments that you provide. If you write:

```
double x = calculateArea(3.0);
```

Java looks for a method named `calculateArea` that takes one `double` as an argument, and so it uses the first version, which interprets the argument as a radius. If you write:

```
double y = calculateArea(1.0, 2.0, 4.0, 6.0);
```

Java uses the second version of `calculateArea`, which interprets the arguments as two points. In this example, the second version actually invokes the first version.

Many Java methods are overloaded, meaning that there are different versions that accept different numbers or types of parameters. For example, there are versions of `print` and `println` that accept a single parameter of any data type. In the `Math` class, there is a version of `abs` that works on `doubles`, and there is also a version for `ints`.

Although overloading is a useful feature, it should be used with caution. You might get yourself nicely confused if you are trying to debug one version of a method while accidentally invoking a different one.

Boolean Methods

Methods can return `boolean` values, just like any other type, which is often convenient for hiding tests inside methods. For example:

```
public static boolean isSingleDigit(int x) {
    if (x > -10 && x < 10) {
        return true;
    } else {
        return false;
    }
}
```

The name of this method is `isSingleDigit`. It is common to give `boolean` methods names that sound like yes/no questions. Since the return type is `boolean`, the return statement has to provide a boolean expression.

The code itself is straightforward, although it is longer than it needs to be. Remember that the expression `x > -10 && x < 10` has type `boolean`, so there is nothing wrong with returning it directly (without the `if` statement):

```
public static boolean isSingleDigit(int x) {
    return x > -10 && x < 10;
}
```

In `main`, you can invoke the method in the usual ways:

```
System.out.println(isSingleDigit(2));
boolean bigFlag = !isSingleDigit(17);
```

The first line displays `true` because 2 is a single-digit number. The second line sets `bigFlag` to `true`, because 17 is *not* a single-digit number.

Conditional statements often invoke `boolean` methods and use the result as the condition:

```
if (isSingleDigit(z)) {
    System.out.println("z is small");
} else {
    System.out.println("z is big");
}
```

Examples like this one almost read like English: "If is single digit z, print ... else print ...".

Javadoc Tags

In "Writing Documentation" on page 53, we discussed how to write documentation comments using /**. It's generally a good idea to document each class and method, so that other programmers can understand what they do without having to read the code.

To organize the documentation into sections, Javadoc supports optional **tags** that begin with the at sign (@). For example, we can use `@param` and `@return` to provide additional information about parameters and return values.

```
/**
 * Tests whether x is a single digit integer.
 *
 * @param x the integer to test
 * @return true if x has one digit, false otherwise
 */
public static boolean isSingleDigit(int x) {
```

Figure 6-1 shows part of the resulting HTML page generated by Javadoc. Notice the relationship between the source code and the documentation.

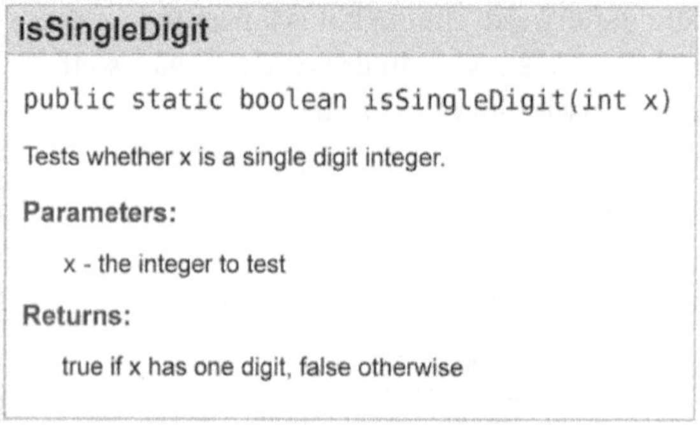

Figure 6-1. HTML documentation for `isSingleDigit`.

Methods with multiple parameters should have separate `@param` tags that describe each one. Void methods should have no `@return` tag, since they do not return a value.

More Recursion

Now that we have methods that return values, we have a **Turing complete** programming language. That means Java can compute anything computable, for any reasonable definition of "computable". This idea was developed by Alonzo Church and Alan Turing, so it is known as the Church-Turing thesis.

To give you an idea of what you can do with the tools we have learned, let's look at some methods for evaluating recursively-defined mathematical functions. A recursive definition is similar to a circular definition, in the sense that the definition refers to the thing being defined.

Of course, a truly circular definition is not very useful:

recursive:
> An adjective used to describe a method that is recursive.

If you saw that definition in the dictionary, you might be annoyed. But if you search for recursion on Google, it displays "Did you mean: recursion" as an inside joke.

Many mathematical functions are defined recursively, because that is often the simplest way. For example, the **factorial** of an integer n, which is written $n!$, is defined like this:

$$0! = 1$$
$$n! = n \cdot (n - 1)!$$

Don't confuse the mathematical symbol !, which means *factorial*, with the Java operator !, which means *not*. This definition says that `factorial(0)` is 1, and that `facto rial(n)` is `n * factorial(n - 1)`.

So `factorial(3)` is `3 * factorial(2)`; `factorial(2)` is `2 * factorial(1)`; `factorial(1)` is `1 * factorial(0)`; and `factorial(0)` is 1. Putting it all together, we get `3 * 2 * 1 * 1`, which is 6.

If you can formulate a recursive definition of something, you can easily write a Java method to evaluate it. The first step is to decide what the parameters and return type are. Since factorial is defined for integers, the method takes an `int` as a parameter and returns an `int`. So here's a good starting place:

```
public static int factorial(int n) {
    return 0;
}
```

Next, we think about the base case. If the argument happens to be zero, we return 1.

```
public static int factorial(int n) {
    if (n == 0) {
        return 1;
    }
    return 0;
}
```

Otherwise, and this is the interesting part, we have to make a recursive call to find the factorial of $n - 1$, and then multiply it by n.

```
public static int factorial(int n) {
    if (n == 0) {
        return 1;
    }
    int recurse = factorial(n - 1);
    int result = n * recurse;
    return result;
}
```

The flow of execution for this program is similar to countdown from "Recursive Methods" on page 62. If we invoke factorial with the value 3:

Since 3 is not zero, we take the second branch and calculate the factorial of $n - 1$...

Since 2 is not zero, we take the second branch and calculate the factorial of $n - 1$...

Since 1 is not zero, we take the second branch and calculate the factorial of $n - 1$...

Since 0 *is* zero, we take the first branch and return the value 1 immediately.

The return value (1) gets multiplied by n, which is 1, and the result is returned.

The return value (1) gets multiplied by n, which is 2, and the result is returned.

The return value (2) gets multiplied by n, which is 3, and the result, 6, is returned to whatever invoked factorial(3).

Figure 6-2 shows what the stack diagram looks like for this sequence of method invocations. The return values are shown being passed back up the stack. Notice that recurse and result do not exist in the last frame, because when n == 0 the code that declares them does not execute.

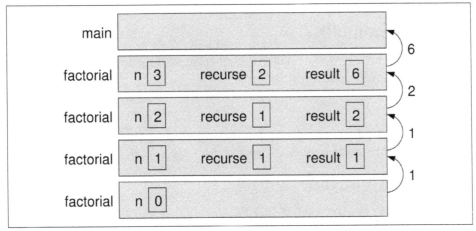

Figure 6-2. Stack diagram for the `factorial` *method.*

Leap of Faith

Following the flow of execution is one way to read programs, but it can quickly become overwhelming. An alternative is the **leap of faith**: when you come to a method invocation, instead of following the flow of execution, you *assume* that the method works correctly and returns the appropriate value.

In fact, you are already practicing a leap of faith when you use methods in the Java library. When you invoke `Math.cos` or `System.out.println`, you don't examine the implementations of those methods. You just assume that they work properly.

You should apply the same reasoning to your own methods. For example, in "Boolean Methods" on page 77 we wrote a method called `isSingleDigit` that determines whether a number is between 0 and 9. Once we convince ourselves that this method is correct—by testing and examination of the code—we can use the method without ever looking at the implementation again.

The same is true of recursive methods. When you get to the recursive call, instead of following the flow of execution you should *assume* that the recursive invocation works. For example, "Assuming that I can find the factorial of $n - 1$, can I compute the factorial of n?" Yes you can, by multiplying by n.

Of course, it is strange to assume that the method works correctly when you have not finished writing it, but that's why it's called a leap of faith!

One More Example

Another common recursively-defined mathematical function is the Fibonacci sequence, which has the following definition:

$$fibonacci(1) = 1$$
$$fibonacci(2) = 1$$
$$fibonacci(n) = fibonacci(n-1) + fibonacci(n-2)$$

Translated into Java, this function is:

```java
public static int fibonacci(int n) {
    if (n == 1 || n == 2) {
        return 1;
    }
    return fibonacci(n - 1) + fibonacci(n - 2);
}
```

If you try to follow the flow of execution here, even for small values of n, your head will explode. But if we take a leap of faith and assume that the two recursive invocations work correctly, it is clear that their sum is the result.

Vocabulary

void method:
> A method that does not return a value.

value method:
> A method that returns a value.

return type:
> The type of value a method returns.

return value:
> The value provided as the result of a method invocation.

temporary variable:
> A short-lived variable, often used for debugging.

dead code:
> Part of a program that can never be executed, often because it appears after a return statement.

incremental development:
> A process for creating programs by writing a few lines at a time, compiling, and testing.

stub:
>A placeholder for an incomplete method so that the class will compile.

scaffolding:
>Code that is used during program development but is not part of the final version.

functional decomposition:
>A process for breaking down a complex computation into simple methods, then composing the methods to perform the computation.

overload:
>To define more than one method with the same name but different parameters.

tag:
>A label that begins with an at sign (@) and is used by Javadoc to organize documentation into sections.

Turing complete:
>A programming language that can implement any theoretically possible algorithm.

factorial:
>The product of all the integers up to and including a given integer.

leap of faith:
>A way to read recursive programs by assuming that the recursive call works, rather than following the flow of execution.

Exercises

The code for this chapter is in the ch06 directory of ThinkJavaCode. See "Using the Code Examples" on page xi for instructions on how to download the repository. Before you start the exercises, we recommend that you compile and run the examples.

If you have not already read "Testing with JUnit" on page 208, now might be a good time. It describes JUnit, a tool for efficiently testing value methods.

Exercise 6-1.

If you have a question about whether something is legal, and what happens if it is not, a good way to find out is to ask the compiler. Answer the following questions by trying them out.

1. What happens if you invoke a value method and don't do anything with the result; that is, if you don't assign it to a variable or use it as part of a larger expression?

2. What happens if you use a void method as part of an expression? For example, try `System.out.println("boo!") + 7;`

Exercise 6-2.

Write a method named `isDivisible` that takes two integers, n and m, and that returns `true` if n is divisible by m, and `false` otherwise.

Exercise 6-3.

If you are given three sticks, you may or may not be able to arrange them in a triangle. For example, if one of the sticks is 12 inches long and the other two are one inch long, you will not be able to get the short sticks to meet in the middle. For any three lengths, there is a simple test to see if it is possible to form a triangle:

> If any of the three lengths is greater than the sum of the other two, you cannot form a triangle.

Write a method named `isTriangle` that takes three integers as arguments and returns either `true` or `false`, depending on whether you can or cannot form a triangle from sticks with the given lengths. The point of this exercise is to use conditional statements to write a value method.

Exercise 6-4.

Many computations can be expressed more concisely using the "multadd" operation, which takes three operands and computes a * b + c. Some processors even provide a hardware implementation of this operation for floating-point numbers.

1. Create a new program called `Multadd.java`.

2. Write a method called `multadd` that takes three `doubles` as parameters and that returns a * b + c.

3. Write a `main` method that tests `multadd` by invoking it with a few simple parameters, like `1.0, 2.0, 3.0`.

4. Also in `main`, use `multadd` to compute the following values:

$$\sin \frac{\pi}{4} + \frac{\cos \frac{\pi}{4}}{2}$$

$$\log 10 + \log 20$$

5. Write a method called `expSum` that takes a double as a parameter and that uses `multadd` to calculate:

$$xe^{-x} + \sqrt{1 - e^{-x}}$$

Hint: The method for raising *e* to a power is `Math.exp`.

In the last part of this exercise, you need to write a method that invokes another method you wrote. Whenever you do that, it is a good idea to test the first method carefully before working on the second. Otherwise, you might find yourself debugging two methods at the same time, which can be difficult.

One of the purposes of this exercise is to practice pattern-matching: the ability to recognize a specific problem as an instance of a general category of problems.

Exercise 6-5.

What is the output of the following program?

```
public static void main(String[] args) {
    boolean flag1 = isHoopy(202);
    boolean flag2 = isFrabjuous(202);
    System.out.println(flag1);
    System.out.println(flag2);
    if (flag1 && flag2) {
        System.out.println("ping!");
    }
    if (flag1 || flag2) {
        System.out.println("pong!");
    }
}
public static boolean isHoopy(int x) {
    boolean hoopyFlag;
    if (x % 2 == 0) {
        hoopyFlag = true;
    } else {
        hoopyFlag = false;
    }
    return hoopyFlag;
}
```

```
public static boolean isFrabjuous(int x) {
    boolean frabjuousFlag;
    if (x > 0) {
        frabjuousFlag = true;
    } else {
        frabjuousFlag = false;
    }
    return frabjuousFlag;
}
```

The purpose of this exercise is to make sure you understand logical operators and the flow of execution through value methods.

Exercise 6-6.

In this exercise, you will use a stack diagram to understand the execution of the following recursive program.

```
public static void main(String[] args) {
    System.out.println(prod(1, 4));
}

public static int prod(int m, int n) {
    if (m == n) {
        return n;
    } else {
        int recurse = prod(m, n - 1);
        int result = n * recurse;
        return result;
    }
}
```

1. Draw a stack diagram showing the state of the program just before the last invocation of prod completes.

2. What is the output of this program? (Try to answer this question on paper first, then run the code to check your answer.)

3. Explain in a few words what prod does (without getting into the details of how it works).

4. Rewrite prod without the temporary variables recurse and result. *Hint:* You only need one line for the else branch.

Exercise 6-7.

Write a recursive method named oddSum that takes a positive odd integer n and returns the sum of odd integers from 1 to n. Start with a base case, and use temporary variables to debug your solution. You might find it helpful to print the value of n each time oddSum is invoked.

Exercise 6-8.

The goal of this exercise is to translate a recursive definition into a Java method. The Ackermann function is defined for non-negative integers as follows:

$$A(m, n) = \begin{cases} n + 1 & \text{if } m = 0 \\ A(m - 1, 1) & \text{if } m > 0 \text{ and } n = 0 \\ A(m - 1, A(m, n - 1)) & \text{if } m > 0 \text{ and } n > 0 \end{cases}$$

Write a method called ack that takes two ints as parameters and that computes and returns the value of the Ackermann function.

Test your implementation of Ackermann by invoking it from main and displaying the return value. Note the return value gets very big very quickly. You should try it only for small values of *m* and *n* (not bigger than 3).

Exercise 6-9.

Write a recursive method called power that takes a double x and an integer n and returns x^n.

Hint: A recursive definition of this operation is $x^n = x \cdot x^{n-1}$. Also, remember that anything raised to the zeroth power is 1.

Optional challenge: you can make this method more efficient, when n is even, using $x^n = \left(x^{n/2}\right)^2$.

CHAPTER 7

Loops

Computers are often used to automate repetitive tasks. Repeating tasks without making errors is something that computers do well and people do poorly.

Running the same code multiple times is called **iteration**. We have seen methods, like countdown and factorial, that use recursion to iterate. Although recursion is elegant and powerful, it takes some getting used to. Java provides language features that make iteration much easier: the while and for statements.

The while Statement

Using a while statement, we can rewrite countdown like this:

```
public static void countdown(int n) {
    while (n > 0) {
        System.out.println(n);
        n = n - 1;
    }
    System.out.println("Blastoff!");
}
```

You can almost read the while statement like English: "While n is greater than zero, print the value of n and then reduce the value of n by 1. When you get to zero, print Blastoff!"

The expression in parentheses is called the condition. The statements in braces are called the **body**. The flow of execution for a while statement is:

1. Evaluate the condition, yielding true or false.

2. If the condition is false, skip the body and go to the next statement.

3. If the condition is true, execute the body and go back to step 1.

This type of flow is called a **loop**, because the last step loops back around to the first.

The body of the loop should change the value of one or more variables so that, eventually, the condition becomes `false` and the loop terminates. Otherwise the loop will repeat forever, which is called an **infinite loop**. An endless source of amusement for computer scientists is the observation that the directions on shampoo, "Lather, rinse, repeat," are an infinite loop.

In the case of `countdown`, we can prove that the loop terminates when n is positive. But in general, it is not so easy to tell whether a loop terminates. For example, this loop continues until n is 1 (which makes the condition `false`):

```java
public static void sequence(int n) {
    while (n != 1) {
        System.out.println(n);
        if (n % 2 == 0) {          // n is even
            n = n / 2;
        } else {                   // n is odd
            n = n * 3 + 1;
        }
    }
}
```

Each time through the loop, the program displays the value of n and then checks whether it is even or odd. If it is even, the value of n is divided by two. If it is odd, the value is replaced by $3n + 1$. For example, if the starting value (the argument passed to `sequence`) is 3, the resulting sequence is 3, 10, 5, 16, 8, 4, 2, 1.

Since n sometimes increases and sometimes decreases, there is no obvious proof that n will ever reach 1 and that the program will ever terminate. For some values of n, we can prove that it terminates. For example, if the starting value is a power of two, then the value of n will be even every time through the loop until we get to 1. The previous example ends with such a sequence, starting when n is 16.

The hard question is whether this program terminates for *all* values of n. So far, no one has been able to prove it *or* disprove it! For more information, see *https://en.wiki pedia.org/wiki/Collatz_conjecture*.

Generating Tables

Loops are good for generating and displaying tabular data. Before computers were readily available, people had to calculate logarithms, sines and cosines, and other common mathematical functions by hand. To make that easier, there were books of tables where you could look up values of various functions. Creating these tables by hand was slow and boring, and the results were often full of errors.

When computers appeared on the scene, one of the initial reactions was: "This is great! We can use a computer to generate the tables, so there will be no errors." That turned out to be true (mostly), but shortsighted. Not much later, computers were so pervasive that printed tables became obsolete.

Even so, for some operations, computers use tables of values to get an approximate answer, and then perform computations to improve the approximation. In some cases, there have been errors in the underlying tables, most famously in the table the original Intel Pentium used to perform floating-point division (see *https://en.wikipedia.org/wiki/Pentium_FDIV_bug*).

Although a "log table" is not as useful as it once was, it still makes a good example of iteration. The following loop displays a table with a sequence of values in the left column and their logarithms in the right column:

```
int i = 1;
while (i < 10) {
    double x = i;
    System.out.println(x + "   " + Math.log(x));
    i = i + 1;
}
```

The output of this program is:

```
1.0    0.0
2.0    0.6931471805599453
3.0    1.0986122886681098
4.0    1.3862943611198906
5.0    1.6094379124341003
6.0    1.791759469228055
7.0    1.9459101490553132
8.0    2.0794415416798357
9.0    2.1972245773362196
```

Math.log computes natural logarithms, that is, logarithms base *e*. For computer science applications, we often want logarithms with respect to base 2. To compute them, we can apply this equation:

$$\log_2 x = \frac{\log_e x}{\log_e 2}$$

We can modify the loop as follows:

```
int i = 1;
while (i < 10) {
    double x = i;
    System.out.println(x + "   " + Math.log(x) / Math.log(2));
    i = i + 1;
}
```

And here are the results:

```
1.0    0.0
2.0    1.0
3.0    1.5849625007211563
4.0    2.0
5.0    2.321928094887362
6.0    2.584962500721156
7.0    2.807354922057604
8.0    3.0
9.0    3.1699250014423126
```

Each time through the loop, we add one to x, so the result is an arithmetic sequence. If we multiply x by something instead, we get a geometric sequence:

```java
final double LOG2 = Math.log(2);
int i = 1;
while (i < 100) {
    double x = i;
    System.out.println(x + "    " + Math.log(x) / LOG2);
    i = i * 2;
}
```

The first line stores `Math.log(2)` in a `final` variable to avoid computing that value over and over again. The last line multiplies x by 2. The result is:

```
1.0    0.0
2.0    1.0
4.0    2.0
8.0    3.0
16.0   4.0
32.0   5.0
64.0   6.0
```

This table shows the powers of two and their logarithms, base 2. Log tables may not be useful anymore, but for computer scientists, knowing the powers of two helps a lot!

Encapsulation and Generalization

In "Writing Methods" on page 73, we presented a way of writing programs called incremental development. In this section we present another **program development** process called "encapsulation and generalization". The steps are:

1. Write a few lines of code in `main` or another method, and test them.

2. When they are working, wrap them in a new method, and test again.

3. If it's appropriate, replace literal values with variables and parameters.

The second step is called **encapsulation**; the third step is **generalization**.

To demonstrate this process, we'll develop methods that display multiplication tables. Here is a loop that displays the multiples of two, all on one line:

```java
int i = 1;
while (i <= 6) {
    System.out.printf("%4d", 2 * i);
    i = i + 1;
}
System.out.println();
```

The first line initializes a variable named i, which is going to act as a **loop variable**: as the loop executes, the value of i increases from 1 to 6; when i is 7, the loop terminates.

Each time through the loop, we display the value 2 * i padded with spaces so it's four characters wide. Since we use System.out.printf, the output appears on a single line.

After the loop, we call println to print a newline and complete the line. Remember that in some environments, none of the output is displayed until the line is complete.

The output of the code so far is:

```
   2   4   6   8  10  12
```

The next step is to "encapsulate" this code in a new method. Here's what it looks like:

```java
public static void printRow() {
    int i = 1;
    while (i <= 6) {
        System.out.printf("%4d", 2 * i);
        i = i + 1;
    }
    System.out.println();
}
```

Next we replace the constant value, 2, with a parameter, n. This step is called "generalization" because it makes the method more general (less specific).

```java
public static void printRow(int n) {
    int i = 1;
    while (i <= 6) {
        System.out.printf("%4d", n * i);
        i = i + 1;
    }
    System.out.println();
}
```

Invoking this method with the argument 2 yields the same output as before. With the argument 3, the output is:

```
   3   6   9  12  15  18
```

And with argument 4, the output is:

```
4   8  12  16  20  24
```

By now you can probably guess how we are going to display a multiplication table: we'll invoke `printRow` repeatedly with different arguments. In fact, we'll use another loop to iterate through the rows.

```
int i = 1;
while (i <= 6) {
    printRow(i);
    i = i + 1;
}
```

And the output looks like this:

```
1   2   3   4   5   6
2   4   6   8  10  12
3   6   9  12  15  18
4   8  12  16  20  24
5  10  15  20  25  30
6  12  18  24  30  36
```

The format specifier `%4d` in `printRow` causes the output to align vertically, regardless of whether the numbers are one or two digits.

Finally, we encapsulate the second loop in a method:

```
public static void printTable() {
    int i = 1;
    while (i <= 6) {
        printRow(i);
        i = i + 1;
    }
}
```

One of the challenges of programming, especially for beginners, is figuring out how to divide up a program into methods. The process of encapsulation and generalization allows you to design as you go along.

More Generalization

The previous version of `printTable` always displays six rows. We can generalize it by replacing the literal 6 with a parameter:

```
public static void printTable(int rows) {
    int i = 1;
    while (i <= rows) {
        printRow(i);
        i = i + 1;
    }
}
```

Here is the output with the argument 7:

```
1   2   3   4   5   6
2   4   6   8  10  12
3   6   9  12  15  18
4   8  12  16  20  24
5  10  15  20  25  30
6  12  18  24  30  36
7  14  21  28  35  42
```

That's better, but it still has a problem: it always displays the same number of columns. We can generalize more by adding a parameter to printRow:

```java
public static void printRow(int n, int cols) {
    int i = 1;
    while (i <= cols) {
        System.out.printf("%4d", n * i);
        i = i + 1;
    }
    System.out.println();
}
```

Now printRow takes two parameters: n is the value whose multiples should be displayed, and cols is the number of columns. Since we added a parameter to printRow, we also have to change the line in printTable where it is invoked:

```java
public static void printTable(int rows) {
    int i = 1;
    while (i <= rows) {
        printRow(i, rows);
        i = i + 1;
    }
}
```

When this line executes, it evaluates rows and passes the value, which is 7 in this example, as an argument. In printRow, this value is assigned to cols. As a result, the number of columns equals the number of rows, so we get a square 7x7 table:

```
1   2   3   4   5   6   7
2   4   6   8  10  12  14
3   6   9  12  15  18  21
4   8  12  16  20  24  28
5  10  15  20  25  30  35
6  12  18  24  30  36  42
7  14  21  28  35  42  49
```

When you generalize a method appropriately, you often find that it has capabilities you did not plan. For example, you might notice that the multiplication table is symmetric; since $ab = ba$, all the entries in the table appear twice. You could save ink by printing half of the table, and you would only have to change one line of printTable:

```java
printRow(i, i);
```

In words, the length of each row is the same as its row number. The result is a triangular multiplication table.

```
1
2   4
3   6   9
4   8   12  16
5   10  15  20  25
6   12  18  24  30  36
7   14  21  28  35  42  49
```

Generalization makes code more versatile, more likely to be reused, and sometimes easier to write.

The for Statement

The loops we have written so far have several elements in common. They start by initializing a variable, they have a condition that depends on that variable, and inside the loop they do something to update that variable. This type of loop is so common that there is another statement, the for loop, that expresses it more concisely.

For example, we could rewrite printTable like this:

```java
public static void printTable(int rows) {
    for (int i = 1; i <= rows; i = i + 1) {
        printRow(i, rows);
    }
}
```

for loops have three components in parentheses, separated by semicolons: the initializer, the condition, and the update.

1. The *initializer* runs once at the very beginning of the loop.
2. The *condition* is checked each time through the loop. If it is false, the loop ends. Otherwise, the body of the loop is executed (again).
3. At the end of each iteration, the *update* runs, and we go back to step 2.

The for loop is often easier to read because it puts all the loop-related statements at the top of the loop.

There is one difference between for loops and while loops: if you declare a variable in the initializer, it only exists inside the for loop. For example, here is a version of printRow that uses a for loop:

```java
public static void printRow(int n, int cols) {
    for (int i = 1; i <= cols; i = i + 1) {
        System.out.printf("%4d", n * i);
    }
    System.out.println(i);  // compiler error
}
```

The last line tries to display i (for no reason other than demonstration) but it won't work. If you need to use a loop variable outside the loop, you have to declare it outside the loop, like this:

```java
public static void printRow(int n, int cols) {
    int i;
    for (i = 1; i <= cols; i = i + 1) {
        System.out.printf("%4d", n * i);
    }
    System.out.println(i);
}
```

Assignments like i = i + 1 don't often appear in for loops, because Java provides a more concise way to add and subtract by one. Specifically, ++ is the **increment** operator; it has the same effect as i = i + 1. And -- is the **decrement** operator; it has the same effect as i = i - 1.

If you want to increment or decrement a variable by an amount other than 1, you can use += and -=. For example, i += 2 increments i by 2.

The do-while Loop

The while and for statements are **pretest loops**; that is, they test the condition first and at the beginning of each pass through the loop.

Java also provides a **posttest loop**: the do-while statement. This type of loop is useful when you need to run the body of the loop at least once.

For example, in "Validating Input" on page 62 we used the return statement to avoid reading invalid input from the user. We can use a do-while loop to keep reading input until it's valid:

```java
Scanner in = new Scanner(System.in);
boolean okay;
do {
    System.out.print("Enter a number: ");
    if (in.hasNextDouble()) {
        okay = true;
    } else {
        okay = false;
        String word = in.next();
        System.err.println(word + " is not a number");
    }
} while (!okay);
double x = in.nextDouble();
```

Although this code looks complicated, it is essentially only three steps:

1. Display a prompt.

2. Check the input; if invalid, display an error and start over.

3. Read the input.

The code uses a flag variable, okay, to indicate whether we need to repeat the loop body. If hasNextDouble() returns false, we consume the invalid input by calling next(). We then display an error message via System.err. The loop terminates when hasNextDouble() return true.

break and continue

Sometimes neither a pretest nor a posttest loop will provide exactly what you need. In the previous example, the "test" needed to happen in the middle of the loop. As a result, we used a flag variable and a nested if-else statement.

A simpler way to solve this problem is to use a break statement. When a program reaches a break statement, it exits the current loop.

```
Scanner in = new Scanner(System.in);
while (true) {
    System.out.print("Enter a number: ");
    if (in.hasNextDouble()) {
        break;
    }
    String word = in.next();
    System.err.println(word + " is not a number");
}
double x = in.nextDouble();
```

Using true as a conditional in a while loop is an idiom that means "loop forever", or in this case "loop until you get to a break statement."

In addition to the break statement, which exits the loop, Java provides a continue statement that moves on to the next iteration. For example, the following code reads integers from the keyboard and computes a running total. The continue statement causes the program to skip over any negative values.

```
Scanner in = new Scanner(System.in);
int x = -1;
int sum = 0;
while (x != 0) {
    x = in.nextInt();
    if (x <= 0) {
        continue;
    }
    System.out.println("Adding " + x);
    sum += x;
}
```

Although break and continue statements give you more control of the loop execution, they can make code difficult to understand and debug. Use them sparingly.

Vocabulary

iteration:
>   Executing a sequence of statements repeatedly.

loop:
>   A statement that executes a sequence of statements repeatedly.

loop body:
>   The statements inside the loop.

infinite loop:
>   A loop whose condition is always true.

program development:
>   A process for writing programs. So far we have seen "incremental development" and "encapsulation and generalization".

encapsulate:
>   To wrap a sequence of statements in a method.

generalize:
>   To replace something unnecessarily specific (like a constant value) with something appropriately general (like a variable or parameter).

loop variable:
>   A variable that is initialized, tested, and updated in order to control a loop.

increment:
>   Increase the value of a variable.

decrement:
>   Decrease the value of a variable.

pretest loop:
>   A loop that tests the condition before each iteration.

posttest loop:
>   A loop that tests the condition after each iteration.

Exercises

The code for this chapter is in the ch07 directory of ThinkJavaCode. See "Using the Code Examples" on page xi for instructions on how to download the repository.

Before you start the exercises, we recommend that you compile and run the examples.

If you have not already read "Running Checkstyle" on page 206, now might be a good time. It describes Checkstyle, a tool that analyzes many aspects of your source code.

Exercise 7-1.

Consider the following methods:

```
public static void main(String[] args) {
    loop(10);
}

public static void loop(int n) {
    int i = n;
    while (i > 1) {
        System.out.println(i);
        if (i % 2 == 0) {
            i = i / 2;
        } else {
            i = i + 1;
        }
    }
}
```

1. Draw a table that shows the value of the variables i and n during the execution of `loop`. The table should contain one column for each variable and one line for each iteration.

2. What is the output of this program?

3. Can you prove that this loop terminates for any positive value of n?

Exercise 7-2.

Let's say you are given a number, a, and you want to find its square root. One way to do that is to start with a rough guess about the answer, x_0, and then improve the guess using this formula:

$$x_1 = (x_0 + a/x_0)/2$$

For example, if we want to find the square root of 9, and we start with $x_0 = 6$, then $x_1 = (6 + 9/6)/2 = 3.75$, which is closer. We can repeat the procedure, using x_1 to calculate x_2, and so on. In this case, $x_2 = 3.075$ and $x_3 = 3.00091$. So it converges quickly on the correct answer.

Write a method called squareRoot that takes a double and returns an approximation of the square root of the parameter, using this technique. You should not use Math.sqrt.

As your initial guess, you should use $a/2$. Your method should iterate until it gets two consecutive estimates that differ by less than 0.0001. You can use Math.abs to calculate the absolute value of the difference.

Exercise 7-3.

In Exercise 6-9 we wrote a recursive version of power, which takes a double x and an integer n and returns x^n. Now write an iterative method to perform the same calculation.

Exercise 7-4.

"More Recursion" on page 79 presents a recursive method that computes the factorial function. Write an iterative version of factorial.

Exercise 7-5.

One way to calculate e^x is to use the infinite series expansion:

$$e^x = 1 + x + x^2/2! + x^3/3! + x^4/4! + \ldots$$

The ith term in the series is $x^i/i!$.

1. Write a method called myexp that takes x and n as parameters and estimates e^x by adding the first n terms of this series. You can use the factorial method from "More Recursion" on page 79 or your iterative version from the previous exercise.

2. You can make this method more efficient if you realize that the numerator of each term is the same as its predecessor multiplied by x, and the denominator is the same as its predecessor multiplied by i. Use this observation to eliminate the use of Math.pow and factorial, and check that you get the same result.

3. Write a method called check that takes a parameter, x, and displays x, myexp(x), and Math.exp(x). The output should look something like:

```
1.0     2.708333333333333     2.718281828459045
```

You can use the escape sequence "\t" to put a tab character between columns of a table.

4. Vary the number of terms in the series (the second argument that check sends to myexp) and see the effect on the accuracy of the result. Adjust this value until the estimated value agrees with the correct answer when x is 1.

5. Write a loop in main that invokes check with the values 0.1, 1.0, 10.0, and 100.0. How does the accuracy of the result vary as x varies? Compare the number of digits of agreement rather than the difference between the actual and estimated values.

6. Add a loop in main that checks myexp with the values -0.1, -1.0, -10.0, and -100.0. Comment on the accuracy.

Exercise 7-6.

One way to evaluate $\exp\left(-x^2\right)$ is to use the infinite series expansion:

$$\exp\left(-x^2\right) = 1 - x^2 + x^4/2 - x^6/6 + \ldots$$

The ith term in this series is $(-1)^i x^{2i}/i!$. Write a method named gauss that takes x and n as arguments and returns the sum of the first n terms of the series. You should not use factorial or pow.

CHAPTER 8

Arrays

Up to this point, the only variables we have used were for individual values such as numbers or strings. In this chapter, we'll learn how to store multiple values of the same type using a single variable. This language feature will enable you to write programs that manipulate larger amounts of data.

Creating Arrays

An **array** is a sequence of values; the values in the array are called **elements**. You can make an array of ints, doubles, or any other type, but all the values in an array must have the same type.

To create an array, you have to declare a variable with an *array type* and then create the array itself. Array types look like other Java types, except they are followed by square brackets ([ ]). For example, the following lines declare that counts is an "integer array" and values is a "double array":

```
int[] counts;
double[] values;
```

To create the array itself, you have to use the new operator, which we first saw in "The Scanner Class" on page 30:

```
counts = new int[4];
values = new double[size];
```

The first assignment makes count refer to an array of four integers. The second makes values refer to an array of double, where the number of elements in values depends on the value of size.

Of course, you can also declare the variable and create the array in a single line of code:

```
int[] counts = new int[4];
double[] values = new double[size];
```

You can use any integer expression for the size of an array, as long as the value is non-negative. If you try to create an array with −4 elements, for example, you will get a `NegativeArraySizeException`. An array with zero elements is allowed, and there are special uses for such arrays that we'll see later on.

Accessing Elements

When you create an array of `int`s, the elements are initialized to zero. Figure 8-1 shows a state diagram of the `counts` array so far.

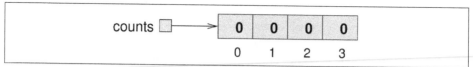

Figure 8-1. State diagram of an int array.

The arrow indicates that the value of `counts` is a **reference** to the array. You should think of *the array* and *the variable* that refers to it as two different things. As we'll soon see, we can assign a different variable to refer to the same array, and we can change the value of `counts` to refer to a different array.

The large numbers inside the boxes are the elements of the array. The small numbers outside the boxes are the **indexes** (or indices) used to identify each location in the array. Notice that the index of the first element is 0, not 1, as you might have expected.

The [ ] operator selects elements from an array:

```
System.out.println("The zeroth element is " + counts[0]);
```

You can use the [ ] operator anywhere in an expression:

```
counts[0] = 7;
counts[1] = counts[0] * 2;
counts[2]++;
counts[3] -= 60;
```

Figure 8-2 shows the result of these statements.

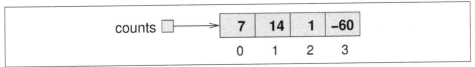

Figure 8-2. State diagram after several assignment statements.

You can use any expression as an index, as long as it has type `int`. One of the most common ways to index an array is with a loop variable. For example:

```
int i = 0;
while (i < 4) {
    System.out.println(counts[i]);
    i++;
}
```

This `while` loop counts from 0 up to 4. When `i` is 4, the condition fails and the loop terminates. So the body of the loop is only executed when `i` is 0, 1, 2, and 3.

Each time through the loop we use `i` as an index into the array, displaying the `i`th element. This type of array processing is often written using a `for` loop.

```
for (int i = 0; i < 4; i++) {
    System.out.println(counts[i]);
}
```

For the `counts` array, the only legal indexes are 0, 1, 2, and 3. If the index is negative or greater than 3, the result is an `ArrayIndexOutOfBoundsException`.

Displaying Arrays

You can use `println` to display an array, but it probably doesn't do what you would like. For example, the following fragment (1) declares an array variable, (2) makes it refer to an array of four elements, and (3) attempts to display the contents of the array using `println`:

```
int[] a = {1, 2, 3, 4};
System.out.println(a);
```

Unfortunately, the output is something like:

```
[I@bf3f7e0
```

The bracket indicates that the value is an array, `I` stands for "integer", and the rest represents the address of the array. If we want to display the elements of the array, we can do it ourselves:

```
public static void printArray(int[] a) {
    System.out.print("{" + a[0]);
    for (int i = 1; i < a.length; i++) {
        System.out.print(", " + a[i]);
    }
    System.out.println("}");
}
```

Given the previous array, the output of this method is:

```
{1, 2, 3, 4}
```

The Java library provides a utility class `java.util.Arrays` that provides methods for working with arrays. One of them, `toString`, returns a string representation of an array. We can invoke it like this:

```
System.out.println(Arrays.toString(a));
```

And the output is:

```
[1, 2, 3, 4]
```

As usual, we have to import `java.util.Arrays` before we can use it. Notice that the string format is slightly different: it uses square brackets instead of curly braces. But it beats having to write the `printArray` method.

Copying Arrays

As explained in "Accessing Elements" on page 104, array variables contain *references* to arrays. When you make an assignment to an array variable, it simply copies the reference. But it doesn't copy the array itself! For example:

```
double[] a = new double[3];
double[] b = a;
```

These statements create an array of three `doubles` and make two different variables refer to it, as shown in Figure 8-3.

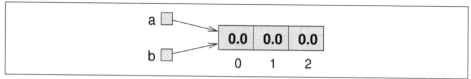

Figure 8-3. State diagram showing two variables that refer to the same array.

Any changes made through either variable will be seen by the other. For example, if we set `a[0]` = `17.0`, and then display `b[0]`, the result is `17.0`. Because `a` and `b` are different names for the same thing, they are sometimes called **aliases**.

If you actually want to copy the array, not just a reference, you have to create a new array and copy the elements from the old to the new, like this:

```
double[] b = new double[3];
for (int i = 0; i < 3; i++) {
    b[i] = a[i];
}
```

Another option is to use `java.util.Arrays`, which provides a method named `copyOf` that copies an array. You can invoke it like this:

```
double[] b = Arrays.copyOf(a, 3);
```

The second parameter is the number of elements you want to copy, so you can also use `copyOf` to copy just part of an array.

Array Length

The examples in the previous section only work if the array has three elements. It would be better to generalize the code to work with arrays of any size. We can do that by replacing the magic number, 3, with `a.length`:

```
double[] b = new double[a.length];
for (int i = 0; i < a.length; i++) {
    b[i] = a[i];
}
```

All arrays have a built-in constant, `length`, that stores the number of elements. The expression `a.length` may look like a method invocation, but there are no parentheses and no arguments.

The last time this loop gets executed, `i` is `a.length - 1`, which is the index of the last element. When `i` is equal to `a.length`, the condition fails and the body is not executed—which is a good thing, because trying to access `a[a.length]` would throw an exception.

You can also use `a.length` with `Arrays.copyOf`:

```
double[] b = Arrays.copyOf(a, a.length);
```

Array Traversal

Many computations can be implemented by looping through the elements of an array and performing an operation on each element. For example, the following loop squares the elements of a `double` array:

```
for (int i = 0; i < a.length; i++) {
    a[i] = Math.pow(a[i], 2.0);
}
```

Looping through the elements of an array is called a **traversal**. Another common pattern is a **search**, which involves traversing an array looking for a particular element.

For example, the following method takes an `int` array and an integer value, and it returns the index where the value appears:

```java
public static int search(double[] a, double target) {
    for (int i = 0; i < a.length; i++) {
        if (a[i] == target) {
            return i;
        }
    }
    return -1;
}
```

If we find the target value in the array, we return its index immediately. If the loop exits without finding the target, it returns -1, a special value chosen to indicate a failed search.

Another common traversal is a **reduce** operation, which "reduces" an array of values down to a single value. Examples include the sum or product of the elements, the minimum, and the maximum. The following method takes a `double` array and returns the sum of the elements:

```java
public static double sum(double[] a) {
    double total = 0.0;
    for (int i = 0; i < a.length; i++) {
        total += a[i];
    }
    return total;
}
```

Before the loop, we initialize `total` to zero. Each time through the loop, we update `total` by adding one element from the array. At the end of the loop, `total` contains the sum of the elements. A variable used this way is sometimes called an **accumulator**.

Random Numbers

Most computer programs do the same thing every time they run; programs like that are **deterministic**. Usually determinism is a good thing, since we expect the same calculation to yield the same result. But for some applications, we want the computer to be unpredictable. Games are an obvious example, but there are many others.

Making a program **nondeterministic** turns out to be hard, because it's hard for a computer to generate truly random numbers. But there are algorithms that generate unpredictable sequences called **pseudorandom** numbers. For most applications, they are as good as random.

If you did Exercise 3-4, you have already seen `java.util.Random`, which generates pseudorandom numbers. The method `nextInt` takes an integer argument, n, and returns a random integer between 0 and n - 1 (inclusive).

If you generate a long series of random numbers, every value should appear, at least approximately, the same number of times. One way to test this behavior of `nextInt` is to generate a large number of values, store them in an array, and count the number of times each value occurs.

The following method creates an `int` array and fills it with random numbers between 0 and 99. The argument specifies the size of the array, and the return value is a reference to the new array.

```java
public static int[] randomArray(int size) {
    Random random = new Random();
    int[] a = new int[size];
    for (int i = 0; i < a.length; i++) {
        a[i] = random.nextInt(100);
    }
    return a;
}
```

The following fragment generates an array and displays it using `printArray` from "Displaying Arrays" on page 105:

```java
int numValues = 8;
int[] array = randomArray(numValues);
printArray(array);
```

The output looks like this:

```
{15, 62, 46, 74, 67, 52, 51, 10}
```

If you run it, you will probably get different values.

Traverse and Count

If these values were exam scores—and they would be pretty bad exam scores—the teacher might present them to the class in the form of a **histogram**. In statistics, a histogram is a set of counters that keeps track of the number of times each value appears.

For exam scores, we might have ten counters to keep track of how many students scored in the 90s, the 80s, etc. To do that, we can traverse the array and count the number of elements that fall in a given range.

The following method takes an array and two integers, `low` and `high`. It returns the number of elements that fall in the range from `low` to `high`.

```
public static int inRange(int[] a, int low, int high) {
    int count = 0;
    for (int i = 0; i < a.length; i++) {
        if (a[i] >= low && a[i] < high) {
            count++;
        }
    }
    return count;
}
```

This pattern should look familiar: it is another reduce operation. Notice that low is included in the range (>=), but high is excluded (<). This detail keeps us from counting any scores twice.

Now we can count the number of scores in each grade range:

```
int[] scores = randomArray(30);
int a = inRange(scores, 90, 100);
int b = inRange(scores, 80, 90);
int c = inRange(scores, 70, 80);
int d = inRange(scores, 60, 70);
int f = inRange(scores, 0, 60);
```

Building a Histogram

The previous code is repetitious, but it is acceptable as long as the number of ranges is small. But suppose we wanted to keep track of the number of times each score appears. We would have to write 100 lines of code:

```
int count0 = inRange(scores, 0, 1);
int count1 = inRange(scores, 1, 2);
int count2 = inRange(scores, 2, 3);
...
int count99 = inRange(scores, 99, 100);
```

What we need is a way to store 100 counters, preferably so we can use an index to access them. In other words, we need another array!

The following fragment creates an array of 100 counters, one for each possible score. It loops through the scores and uses inRange to count how many times each score appears. Then it stores the results in the array:

```
int[] counts = new int[100];
for (int i = 0; i < counts.length; i++) {
    counts[i] = inRange(scores, i, i + 1);
}
```

Notice that we are using the loop variable i three times: as an index into the counts array, and as two arguments for inRange. The code works, but it is not as efficient as it could be. Every time the loop invokes inRange, it traverses the entire array.

It would be better to make a single pass through the array, and for each score, compute which range it falls in and increment the corresponding counter. This code traverses the array of scores *only once* to generate the histogram:

```
int[] counts = new int[100];
for (int i = 0; i < scores.length; i++) {
    int index = scores[i];
    counts[index]++;
}
```

Each time through the loop, it selects one element from scores and uses it as an index to increment the corresponding element of counts. Because this code only traverses the array of scores once, it is much more efficient.

The Enhanced for Loop

Since traversing arrays is so common, Java provides an alternative syntax that makes the code more compact. For example, consider a for loop that displays the elements of an array on separate lines:

```
for (int i = 0; i < values.length; i++) {
    int value = values[i];
    System.out.println(value);
}
```

We could rewrite the loop like this:

```
for (int value : values) {
    System.out.println(value);
}
```

This statement is called an **enhanced for loop**. You can read it as, "for each value in values". It's conventional to use plural nouns for array variables and singular nouns for element variables.

Notice how the single line for (int value : values) replaces the first two lines of the standard for loop. It hides the details of iterating each index of the array, and instead, focuses on the values themselves.

Using the enhanced for loop, and removing the temporary variable, we can write the histogram code from the previous section more concisely:

```
int[] counts = new int[100];
for (int score : scores) {
    counts[score]++;
}
```

Enhanced for loops often make the code more readable, especially for accumulating values. But they are not helpful when you need to refer to the index, as in search operations.

Vocabulary

array:
> A collection of values, where all the values have the same type, and each value is identified by an index.

element:
> One of the values in an array. The [ ] operator selects elements.

index:
> An integer variable or value used to indicate an element of an array.

reference:
> A value that indicates another value, like an array. In a state diagram, a reference appears as an arrow.

alias:
> A variable that refers to the same object as another variable.

traversal:
> Looping through the elements of an array (or other collection).

search:
> A traversal pattern used to find a particular element of an array.

reduce:
> A traversal pattern that combines the elements of an array into a single value.

accumulator:
> A variable used to accumulate results during a traversal.

deterministic:
> A program that does the same thing every time it is invoked.

nondeterministic:
> A program that always behaves differently, even when run multiple times with the same input.

pseudorandom:
> A sequence of numbers that appear to be random, but which are actually the product of a deterministic computation.

histogram:
> An array of integers where each integer counts the number of values that fall into a certain range.

enhanced for loop:
> An alternative syntax for traversing the elements (values) of an array.

Exercises

The code for this chapter is in the ch08 directory of ThinkJavaCode. See "Using the Code Examples" on page xi for instructions on how to download the repository. Before you start the exercises, we recommend that you compile and run the examples.

Exercise 8-1.

The goal of this exercise is to practice encapsulation with some of the examples in this chapter.

1. Starting with the code in "Array Traversal" on page 107, write a method called powArray that takes a double array, a, and returns a new array that contains the elements of a squared. Generalize it to take a second argument and raise the elements of a to the given power.

2. Starting with the code in "The Enhanced for Loop" on page 111, write a method called histogram that takes an int array of scores from 0 to (but not including) 100, and returns a histogram of 100 counters. Generalize it to take the number of counters as an argument.

Exercise 8-2.

The purpose of this exercise is to practice reading code and recognizing the traversal patterns in this chapter. The following methods are hard to read, because instead of using meaningful names for the variables and methods, they use names of fruit.

```java
public static int banana(int[] a) {
    int kiwi = 1;
    int i = 0;
    while (i < a.length) {
        kiwi = kiwi * a[i];
        i++;
    }
    return kiwi;
}
public static int grapefruit(int[] a, int grape) {
    for (int i = 0; i < a.length; i++) {
        if (a[i] == grape) {
            return i;
        }
    }
    return -1;
}
```

```
public static int pineapple(int[] a, int apple) {
    int pear = 0;
    for (int pine: a) {
        if (pine == apple) {
            pear++;
        }
    }
    return pear;
}
```

For each method, write one sentence that describes what the method does, without getting into the details of how it works. For each variable, identify the role it plays.

Exercise 8-3.

What is the output of the following program? Draw a stack diagram that shows the state of the program just before mus returns. Describe in a few words what mus does.

```
public static int[] make(int n) {
    int[] a = new int[n];
    for (int i = 0; i < n; i++) {
        a[i] = i + 1;
    }
    return a;
}

public static void dub(int[] jub) {
    for (int i = 0; i < jub.length; i++) {
        jub[i] *= 2;
    }
}

public static int mus(int[] zoo) {
    int fus = 0;
    for (int i = 0; i < zoo.length; i++) {
        fus += zoo[i];
    }
    return fus;
}

public static void main(String[] args) {
    int[] bob = make(5);
    dub(bob);
    System.out.println(mus(bob));
}
```

Exercise 8-4.

Write a method called indexOfMax that takes an array of integers and returns the index of the largest element. Can you write this method using an enhanced for loop? Why or why not?

Exercise 8-5.

The Sieve of Eratosthenes is "a simple, ancient algorithm for finding all prime numbers up to any given limit," which you can read about at *https://en.wikipedia.org/wiki/Sieve_of_Eratosthenes*.

Write a method called `sieve` that takes an integer parameter, n, and returns a `boolean` array that indicates, for each number from 0 to n - 1, whether the number is prime.

Exercise 8-6.

Write a method named `areFactors` that takes an integer n and an array of integers, and that returns `true` if the numbers in the array are all factors of n (which is to say that n is divisible by all of them).

Exercise 8-7.

Write a method named `arePrimeFactors` that takes an integer n and an array of integers, and that returns `true` if the numbers in the array are all prime *and* their product is n.

Exercise 8-8.

Many of the patterns we have seen for traversing arrays can also be written recursively. It is not common, but it is a useful exercise.

1. Write a method called `maxInRange` that takes an array of integers and two indexes, `lowIndex` and `highIndex`, and finds the maximum value in the array, but only considering the elements between `lowIndex` and `highIndex`, including both.

   This method should be recursive. If the length of the range is 1, that is, if `lowIndex == highIndex`, we know immediately that the sole element in the range must be the maximum. So that's the base case.

   If there is more than one element in the range, we can break the array into two pieces, find the maximum in each of the pieces, and then find the maximum of the maxima.

2. Methods like `maxInRange` can be awkward to use. To find the largest element in an array, we have to provide the range for the entire array.

   ```
   double max = maxInRange(a, 0, a.length - 1);
   ```

   Write a method called `max` that takes an array and uses `maxInRange` to find and return the largest element.

CHAPTER 9

Strings and Things

In Java and other object-oriented languages, an **object** is a collection of data that provides a set of methods. For example, `Scanner`, which we saw in "The Scanner Class" on page 30, is an object that provides methods for parsing input. `System.out` and `System.in` are also objects.

Strings are objects, too. They contain characters and provide methods for manipulating character data. We explore some of those methods in this chapter.

Not everything in Java is an object: `int`, `double`, and `boolean` are so-called **primitive** types. We will explain some of the differences between object types and primitive types as we go along.

Characters

Strings provide a method named `charAt`, which extracts a character. It returns a `char`, a primitive type that stores an individual character (as opposed to strings of them).

```
String fruit = "banana";
char letter = fruit.charAt(0);
```

The argument 0 means that we want the letter at position 0. Like array indexes, string indexes start at 0, so the character assigned to `letter` is b.

Characters work like the other primitive types we have seen. You can compare them using relational operators:

```
if (letter == 'a') {
    System.out.println('?');
}
```

Character literals, like `'a'`, appear in single quotes. Unlike string literals, which appear in double quotes, character literals can only contain a single character. Escape sequences, like `'\t'`, are legal because they represent a single character.

The increment and decrement operators work with characters. So this loop displays the letters of the alphabet:

```
System.out.print("Roman alphabet: ");
for (char c = 'A'; c <= 'Z'; c++) {
    System.out.print(c);
}
System.out.println();
```

Java uses **Unicode** to represent characters, so strings can store text in other alphabets like Cyrillic and Greek, and non-alphabetic languages like Chinese. You can read more about it at *http://unicode.org/*.

In Unicode, each character is represented by a "code unit", which you can think of as an integer. The code units for uppercase Greek letters run from 913 to 937, so we can display the Greek alphabet like this:

```
System.out.print("Greek alphabet: ");
for (int i = 913; i <= 937; i++) {
    System.out.print((char) i);
}
System.out.println();
```

This example uses a type cast to convert each integer (in the range) to the corresponding character.

Strings Are Immutable

Strings provide methods, `toUpperCase` and `toLowerCase`, that convert from uppercase to lowercase and back. These methods are often a source of confusion, because it sounds like they modify strings. But neither these methods nor any others can change a string, because strings are **immutable**.

When you invoke `toUpperCase` on a string, you get a new string object as a return value. For example:

```
String name = "Alan Turing";
String upperName = name.toUpperCase();
```

After these statements run, `upperName` refers to the string `"ALAN TURING"`. But `name` still refers to `"Alan Turing"`.

Another useful method is `replace`, which finds and replaces instances of one string within another. This example replaces "Computer Science" with "CS":

```
String text = "Computer Science is fun!";
text = text.replace("Computer Science", "CS");
```

This example demonstrates a common way to work with string methods. It invokes `text.replace`, which returns a reference to a new string, "CS is fun!". Then it assigns the new string to `text`, replacing the old string.

This assignment is important; if you don't save the return value, invoking `text.replace` has no effect.

String Traversal

The following loop traverses the characters in `fruit` and displays them, one on each line:

```
for (int i = 0; i < fruit.length(); i++) {
    char letter = fruit.charAt(i);
    System.out.println(letter);
}
```

Strings provide a method called `length` that returns the number of characters in the string. Because it is a method, you have to invoke it with the empty argument list, `()`.

The condition is `i < fruit.length()`, which means that when `i` is equal to the length of the string, the condition is `false` and the loop terminates.

Unfortunately, the enhanced `for` loop does not work with strings. But you can convert any string to a character array and iterate that:

```
for (char letter : fruit.toCharArray()) {
    System.out.println(letter);
}
```

To find the last letter of a string, you might be tempted to try something like:

```
int length = fruit.length();
char last = fruit.charAt(length);      // wrong!
```

This code compiles and runs, but invoking the `charAt` method throws a `StringIndex OutOfBoundsException`. The problem is that there is no sixth letter in "banana". Since we started counting at 0, the 6 letters are indexed from 0 to 5. To get the last character, you have to subtract 1 from `length`.

```
int length = fruit.length();
char last = fruit.charAt(length - 1); // correct
```

Many string traversals involve reading one string and creating another. For example, to reverse a string, we simply add one character at a time:

```
public static String reverse(String s) {
    String r = "";
    for (int i = s.length() - 1; i >= 0; i--) {
        r = r + s.charAt(i);
    }
    return r;
}
```

The initial value of r is "", which is the **empty string**. The loop traverses the letters of s in reverse order. Each time through the loop, it creates a new string and assigns it to r. When the loop exits, r contains the letters from s in reverse order. So the result of reverse("banana") is "ananab".

Substrings

The substring method returns a new string that copies letters from an existing string, starting at the given index.

- fruit.substring(0) returns "banana"
- fruit.substring(2) returns "nana"
- fruit.substring(6) returns ""

The first example returns a copy of the entire string. The second example returns all but the first two characters. As the last example shows, substring returns the empty string if the argument is the length of the string.

To visualize how the substring method works, it helps to draw a picture like Figure 9-1.

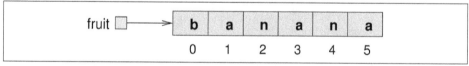

Figure 9-1. State diagram for a String of six characters.

Like most string methods, substring is overloaded. That is, there are other versions of substring that have different parameters. If it's invoked with two arguments, they are treated as a start and end index:

- fruit.substring(0, 3) returns "ban"
- fruit.substring(2, 5) returns "nan"
- fruit.substring(6, 6) returns ""

Notice that the character indicated by the end index is not included. Defining `sub string` this way simplifies some common operations. For example, to select a substring with length `len`, starting at index `i`, you could write `fruit.substring(i, i + len)`.

The indexOf Method

The `indexOf` method searches for a character in a string.

```
String fruit = "banana";
int index = fruit.indexOf('a');
```

This example finds the index of `'a'` in the string. But the letter appears three times, so it's not obvious what `indexOf` should do. According to the documentation, it returns the index of the *first* appearance.

To find subsequent appearances, you can use another version of `indexOf`, which takes a second argument that indicates where in the string to start looking.

```
int index = fruit.indexOf('a', 2);
```

This code starts at index 2 (the first `'n'`) and finds the next `'a'`, which is at index 3. If the letter happens to appear at the starting index, the starting index is the answer. So `fruit.indexOf('a', 5)` returns 5.

If the character does not appear in the string, `indexOf` returns `-1`. Since indexes cannot be negative, this value indicates the character was not found.

You can also use `indexOf` to search for a substring, not just a single character. For example, the expression `fruit.indexOf("nan")` returns 2.

String Comparison

To compare two strings, it may be tempting to use the `==` and `!=` operators.

```
String name1 = "Alan Turing";
String name2 = "Ada Lovelace";
if (name1 == name2) {                    // wrong!
    System.out.println("The names are the same.");
}
```

This code compiles and runs, and most of the time it gets the answer right. But it is not correct, and sometimes it gets the answer wrong. The problem is that the `==` operator checks whether the two variables refer to the same object (by comparing the references). If you give it two different strings that contain the same letters, it yields `false`.

The right way to compare strings is with the `equals` method, like this:

```
if (name1.equals(name2)) {
    System.out.println("The names are the same.");
}
```

This example invokes `equals` on `name1` and passes `name2` as an argument. The `equals` method returns `true` if the strings contain the same characters; otherwise it returns `false`.

If the strings differ, we can use `compareTo` to see which comes first in alphabetical order:

```
int diff = name1.compareTo(name2);
if (diff == 0) {
    System.out.println("The names are the same.");
} else if (diff < 0) {
    System.out.println("name1 comes before name2.");
} else if (diff > 0) {
    System.out.println("name2 comes before name1.");
}
```

The return value from `compareTo` is the difference between the first characters in the strings that differ. If the strings are equal, their difference is zero. If the first string (the one on which the method is invoked) comes first in the alphabet, the difference is negative. Otherwise, the difference is positive.

In the preceding code, `compareTo` returns positive 8, because the second letter of `"Ada"` comes before the second letter of `"Alan"` by 8 letters.

Both `equals` and `compareTo` are case-sensitive. The uppercase letters come before the lowercase letters, so `"Ada"` comes before `"ada"`.

String Formatting

In "Formatting Output" on page 33, we learned how to use `printf` to display formatted output. Sometimes programs need to create strings that are formatted a certain way, but not display them immediately, or ever. For example, the following method returns a time string in 12-hour format:

```
public static String timeString(int hour, int minute) {
    String ampm;
    if (hour < 12) {
        ampm = "AM";
        if (hour == 0) {
            hour = 12;   // midnight
        }
    } else {
        ampm = "PM";
        hour = hour - 12;
    }
    return String.format("%02d:%02d %s", hour, minute, ampm);
}
```

`String.format` takes the same arguments as `System.out.printf`: a format specifier followed by a sequence of values. The main difference is that `System.out.printf` displays the result on the screen; `String.format` creates a new string, but does not display anything.

In this example, the format specifier `%02d` means "two digit integer padded with zeros", so `timeString(19, 5)` returns the string `"07:05 PM"`.

Wrapper Classes

Primitive values (like `int`s, `double`s, and `char`s) do not provide methods. For example, you can't call `equals` on an `int`:

```
int i = 5;
System.out.println(i.equals(5));  // compiler error
```

But for each primitive type, there is a corresponding class in the Java library, called a **wrapper class**. The wrapper class for `char` is called `Character`; for `int` it's called `Integer`. Other wrapper classes include `Boolean`, `Long`, and `Double`. They are in the `java.lang` package, so you can use them without importing them.

Each wrapper class defines constants `MIN_VALUE` and `MAX_VALUE`. For example, `Integer.MIN_VALUE` is `-2147483648`, and `Integer.MAX_VALUE` is `2147483647`. Because these constants are available in wrapper classes, you don't have to remember them, and you don't have to include them in your programs.

Wrapper classes provide methods for converting strings to other types. For example, `Integer.parseInt` converts a string to (you guessed it) an integer:

```
String str = "12345";
int num = Integer.parseInt(str);
```

In this context, **parse** means something like "read and translate".

The other wrapper classes provide similar methods, like `Double.parseDouble` and `Boolean.parseBoolean`. They also provide `toString`, which returns a string representation of a value:

```
int num = 12345;
String str = Integer.toString(num);
```

The result is the string `"12345"`.

Command-Line Arguments

Now that you know about arrays and strings, we can *finally* explain the `args` parameter for `main` that we have been ignoring since Chapter 1. If you are unfamiliar with the command-line interface, please read or review "Command-Line Interface" on page 203.

Continuing an earlier example, let's write a program to find the largest value in a sequence of numbers. Rather than read the numbers from System.in, we'll pass them as command-line arguments. Here is a starting point:

```java
public class Max {
    public static void main(String[] args) {
        System.out.println(Arrays.toString(args));
    }
}
```

You can run this program from the command line by typing:

```
java Max
```

The output indicates that args is an **empty array**; that is, it has no elements:

```
[]
```

But if you provide additional values on the command line, they are passed as arguments to main. For example, if you run it like this:

```
java Max 10 -3 55 0 14
```

The output is:

```
[10, -3, 55, 0, 14]
```

But remember that the elements of args are strings. To find the maximum number, we have to convert the arguments to integers.

The following fragment uses an enhanced for loop to parse the arguments (using the Integer wrapper class) and find the largest value:

```java
int max = Integer.MIN_VALUE;
for (String arg : args) {
    int value = Integer.parseInt(arg);
    if (value > max) {
        max = value;
    }
}
System.out.println("The max is " + max);
```

The initial value of max is the smallest (most negative) number an int can represent, so any other value is greater. If args is empty, the result is MIN_VALUE.

Vocabulary

object:
> A collection of related data that comes with a set of methods that operate on it.

primitive:
> A data type that stores a single value and provides no methods.

Unicode:
> A standard for representing characters in most of the world's languages.

immutable:
> An object that, once created, cannot be modified. Strings are immutable by design.

empty string:
> The string " ", which contains no characters and has a length of zero.

wrapper class:
> Classes in `java.lang` that provide constants and methods for working with primitive types.

parse:
> To read a string and interpret or translate it.

empty array:
> An array with no elements and a length of zero.

Exercises

The code for this chapter is in the `ch09` directory of `ThinkJavaCode`. See "Using the Code Examples" on page xi for instructions on how to download the repository. Before you start the exercises, we recommend that you compile and run the examples.

Exercise 9-1.

The point of this exercise is to explore Java types and fill in some of the details that aren't covered in the chapter.

1. Create a new program named `Test.java` and write a `main` method that contains expressions that combine various types using the + operator. For example, what happens when you "add" a `String` and a `char`? Does it perform character addition or string concatenation? What is the type of the result? (How can you determine the type of the result?)

2. Make a bigger copy of the following table and fill it in. At the intersection of each pair of types, you should indicate whether it is legal to use the + operator with these types, what operation is performed (addition or concatenation), and what the type of the result is.

	boolean	char	int	double	String
boolean					
char					
int					
double					
String					

3. Think about some of the choices the designers of Java made when they filled in this table. How many of the entries seem unavoidable, as if there was no other choice? How many seem like arbitrary choices from several equally reasonable possibilities? Which entries seem most problematic?

4. Here's a puzzler: normally, the statement x++ is exactly equivalent to x = x + 1. But if x is a char, it's not exactly the same! In that case, x++ is legal, but x = x + 1 causes an error. Try it out and see what the error message is, then see if you can figure out what is going on.

5. What happens when you add "" (the empty string) to the other types, for example, "" + 5?

6. For each data type, what types of values can you assign to it? For example, you can assign an int to a double but not vice versa.

Exercise 9-2.

Write a method called letterHist that takes a string as a parameter and returns a histogram of the letters in the string. The zeroth element of the histogram should contain the number of a's in the string (upper- and lowercase); the 25th element should contain the number of z's. Your solution should only traverse the string once.

Exercise 9-3.

The purpose of this exercise is to review encapsulation and generalization (see "Encapsulation and Generalization" on page 92). The following code fragment traverses a string and checks whether it has the same number of open and close parentheses:

```
String s = "((3 + 7) * 2)";
int count = 0;

for (int i = 0; i < s.length(); i++) {
    char c = s.charAt(i);
    if (c == '(') {
        count++;
    } else if (c == ')') {
        count--;
    }
}

System.out.println(count);
```

1. Encapsulate this fragment in a method that takes a string argument and returns the final value of count.

2. Now that you have generalized the code so that it works on any string, what could you do to generalize it more?

3. Test your method with multiple strings, including some that are balanced and some that are not.

Exercise 9-4.

Create a program called Recurse.java and type in the following methods:

```
/**
 * Returns the first character of the given String.
 */
public static char first(String s) {
    return s.charAt(0);
}
/**
 * Returns all but the first letter of the given String.
 */
public static String rest(String s) {
    return s.substring(1);
}
/**
 * Returns all but the first and last letter of the String.
 */
public static String middle(String s) {
    return s.substring(1, s.length() - 1);
}
/**
 * Returns the length of the given String.
 */
public static int length(String s) {
    return s.length();
}
```

1. Write some code in main that tests each of these methods. Make sure they work, and you understand what they do.

2. Using these methods, and without using any other String methods, write a method called printString that takes a string as a parameter and that displays the letters of the string, one on each line. It should be a void method.

3. Again using only these methods, write a method called printBackward that does the same thing as printString but that displays the string backward (again, one character per line).

4. Now write a method called reverseString that takes a string as a parameter and that returns a new string as a return value. The new string should contain the same letters as the parameter, but in reverse order.

```
String backwards = reverseString("coffee");
System.out.println(backwards);
```

The output of this example code should be:

```
eeffoc
```

5. A palindrome is a word that reads the same both forward and backward, like "otto" and "palindromeemordnilap". Here's one way to test whether a string is a palindrome:

> A single letter is a palindrome, a two-letter word is a palindrome if the letters are the same, and any other word is a palindrome if the first letter is the same as the last and the middle is a palindrome.

Write a recursive method named isPalindrome that takes a String and returns a boolean indicating whether the word is a palindrome.

Exercise 9-5.

A word is said to be "abecedarian" if the letters in the word appear in alphabetical order. For example, the following are all six-letter English abecedarian words:

> abdest, acknow, acorsy, adempt, adipsy, agnosy, befist, behint, beknow, bijoux, biopsy, cestuy, chintz, deflux, dehors, dehort, deinos, diluvy, dimpsy

Write a method called isAbecedarian that takes a String and returns a boolean indicating whether the word is abecedarian. Your method can be iterative or recursive.

Exercise 9-6.

A word is said to be a "doubloon" if every letter that appears in the word appears exactly twice. Here are some example doubloons found in the dictionary:

> Abba, Anna, appall, appearer, appeases, arraigning, beriberi, bilabial, boob, Caucasus, coco, Dada, deed, Emmett, Hannah, horseshoer, intestines, Isis, mama, Mimi, murmur, noon, Otto, papa, peep, reappear, redder, sees, Shanghaiings, Toto

Write a method called `isDoubloon` that takes a string and checks whether it is a doubloon. To ignore case, invoke the `toLowerCase` method before checking.

Exercise 9-7.

Two words are anagrams if they contain the same letters and the same number of each letter. For example, "stop" is an anagram of "pots" and "allen downey" is an anagram of "well annoyed".

Write a method that takes two strings and checks whether they are anagrams of each other.

Exercise 9-8.

In Scrabble[1] each player has a set of tiles with letters on them. The object of the game is to use those letters to spell words. The scoring system is complex, but longer words are usually worth more than shorter words.

Imagine you are given your set of tiles as a string, like `"quijibo"`, and you are given another string to test, like `"jib"`.

Write a method called `canSpell` that takes two strings and checks whether the set of tiles can spell the word. You might have more than one tile with the same letter, but you can only use each tile once.

---

1 Scrabble is a registered trademark owned in the USA and Canada by Hasbro Inc., and in the rest of the world by J. W. Spear & Sons Limited of Maidenhead, Berkshire, England, a subsidiary of Mattel Inc.

CHAPTER 10

Objects

As we learned in the previous chapter, an object is a collection of data that provides a set of methods. For example, a `String` is a collection of characters that provides methods like `charAt` and `substring`.

Java is an "object-oriented" language, which means that it uses objects to represent data *and* provide methods related to them. This way of organizing programs is a powerful design concept, and we will introduce it a little at a time throughout the remainder of the book.

In this chapter, we introduce two new types of objects: `Point` and `Rectangle`. We show how to write methods that take objects as parameters and produce objects as return values. We also take a look at the source code for the Java library.

Point Objects

The `java.awt` package provides a class named `Point` intended to represent the coordinates of a location in a Cartesian plane. In mathematical notation, points are often written in parentheses with a comma separating the coordinates. For example, $(0, 0)$ indicates the origin, and (x, y) indicates the point x units to the right and y units up from the origin.

In order to use the `Point` class, you have to import it:

```
import java.awt.Point;
```

Then, to create a new point, you have to use the `new` operator:

```
Point blank;
blank = new Point(3, 4);
```

The first line declares that `blank` has type `Point`. The second line creates the new `Point` with the given arguments as coordinates.

The result of the `new` operator is a *reference* to the new object. So `blank` contains a reference to the new `Point` object. Figure 10-1 shows the result.

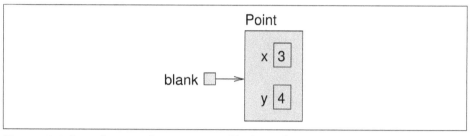

Figure 10-1. State diagram showing a variable that refers to a `Point` object.

As usual, the name of the variable `blank` appears outside the box, and its value appears inside the box. In this case, the value is a reference, which is represented with an arrow. The arrow points to the new object, which contains two variables, x and y.

Attributes

Variables that belong to an object are usually called **attributes**, but you might also see them called "fields". To access an attribute of an object, Java uses **dot notation**. For example:

```java
int x = blank.x;
```

The expression `blank.x` means "go to the object `blank` refers to, and get the value of the attribute x." In this case, we assign that value to a local variable named x. There is no conflict between the local variable named x and the attribute named x. The purpose of dot notation is to identify *which* variable you are referring to unambiguously.

You can use dot notation as part of an expression. For example:

```java
System.out.println(blank.x + ", " + blank.y);
int sum = blank.x * blank.x + blank.y * blank.y;
```

The first line displays 3, 4; the second line calculates the value 25.

Objects as Parameters

You can pass objects as parameters in the usual way. For example:

```
public static void printPoint(Point p) {
    System.out.println("(" + p.x + ", " + p.y + ")");
}
```

This method takes a point as an argument and displays its attributes in parentheses. If you invoke printPoint(blank), it displays (3, 4).

But we don't really need a method like printPoint, because if you invoke System.out.println(blank) you get:

```
java.awt.Point[x=3,y=4]
```

Point objects provide a method called toString that returns a string representation of a point. When you call println with objects, it automatically calls toString and displays the result. In this case, it shows the name of the type (java.awt.Point) and the names and values of the attributes.

As another example, we can rewrite the distance method from "Writing Methods" on page 73 so that it takes two Points as parameters instead of four doubles.

```
public static double distance(Point p1, Point p2) {
    int dx = p2.x - p1.x;
    int dy = p2.y - p1.y;
    return Math.sqrt(dx * dx + dy * dy);
}
```

Passing objects as parameters makes the source code more readable and less error-prone, because related values are bundled together.

Objects as Return Types

The java.awt package also provides a class called Rectangle. To use it, you have to import it:

```
import java.awt.Rectangle;
```

Rectangle objects are similar to points, but they have four attributes: x, y, width, and height. The following example creates a Rectangle object and makes the variable box refer to it:

```
Rectangle box = new Rectangle(0, 0, 100, 200);
```

Figure 10-2 shows the effect of this assignment.

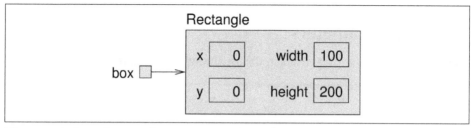

Figure 10-2. State diagram showing a Rectangle object.

If you run System.out.println(box), you get:

```
java.awt.Rectangle[x=0,y=0,width=100,height=200]
```

Again, println uses the toString method provided by Rectangle, which knows how to display Rectangle objects.

You can write methods that return objects. For example, findCenter takes a Rectangle as an argument and returns a Point with the coordinates of the center of the rectangle:

```
public static Point findCenter(Rectangle box) {
    int x = box.x + box.width / 2;
    int y = box.y + box.height / 2;
    return new Point(x, y);
}
```

The return type of this method is Point. The last line creates a new Point object and returns a reference to it.

Mutable Objects

You can change the contents of an object by making an assignment to one of its attributes. For example, to "move" a rectangle without changing its size, you can modify the x and y values:

```
Rectangle box = new Rectangle(0, 0, 100, 200);
box.x = box.x + 50;
box.y = box.y + 100;
```

The result is shown in Figure 10-3.

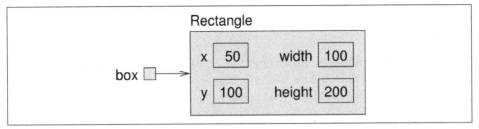

Figure 10-3. State diagram showing updated attributes.

We can encapsulate this code in a method and generalize it to move the rectangle by any amount:

```
public static void moveRect(Rectangle box, int dx, int dy) {
    box.x = box.x + dx;
    box.y = box.y + dy;
}
```

The variables dx and dy indicate how far to move the rectangle in each direction. Invoking this method has the effect of modifying the Rectangle that is passed as an argument.

```
Rectangle box = new Rectangle(0, 0, 100, 200);
moveRect(box, 50, 100);
System.out.println(box);
```

Modifying objects by passing them as arguments to methods can be useful. But it can also make debugging more difficult, because it is not always clear which method invocations modify their arguments.

Java provides a number of methods that operate on Points and Rectangles. For example, translate has the same effect as moveRect, but instead of passing the rectangle as an argument, you use dot notation:

```
box.translate(50, 100);
```

This line invokes the translate method for the object that box refers to. As a result, the box object is updated directly.

This example is a good illustration of **object-oriented** programming. Rather than write methods like moveRect that modify one or more parameters, we apply methods to objects themselves using dot notation.

Aliasing

Remember that when you assign an object to a variable, you are assigning a *reference* to an object. It is possible to have multiple variables that refer to the same object. The state diagram in Figure 10-4 shows the result.

```
Rectangle box1 = new Rectangle(0, 0, 100, 200);
Rectangle box2 = box1;
```

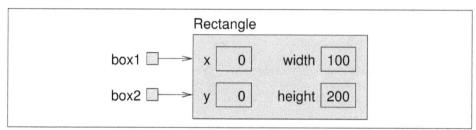

Figure 10-4. State diagram showing two variables that refer to the same object.

Notice how box1 and box2 are aliases for the same object, so any changes that affect one variable also affect the other. This example adds 50 to all four sides of the rectangle, so it moves the corner up and to the left by 50, and it increases the height and width by 100:

```
System.out.println(box2.width);
box1.grow(50, 50);
System.out.println(box2.width);
```

The first line displays 100, which is the width of the Rectangle referred to by box2. The second line invokes the grow method on box1, which stretches the Rectangle horizontally and vertically. The effect is shown in Figure 10-5.

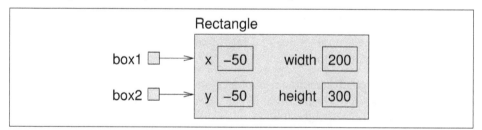

Figure 10-5. State diagram showing the effect of invoking grow.

When we make a change using box1, we see the change using box2. Thus, the value displayed by the third line is 200, the width of the expanded rectangle.

The null Keyword

When you create an object variable, remember that you are storing a reference to an object. In Java, the keyword `null` is a special value that means "no object". You can declare and initialize object variables this way:

```
Point blank = null;
```

The value `null` is represented in state diagrams by a small box with no arrow, as in Figure 10-6.

Figure 10-6. State diagram showing a variable that contains a null reference.

If you try to use a `null` value, either by accessing an attribute or invoking a method, Java throws a `NullPointerException`.

```
Point blank = null;
int x = blank.x;            // NullPointerException
blank.translate(50, 50);    // NullPointerException
```

On the other hand, it is legal to pass a null reference as an argument or receive one as a return value. For example, `null` is often used to represent a special condition or indicate an error.

Garbage Collection

In "Aliasing" on page 136, we saw what happens when more than one variable refers to the same object. What happens when *no* variables refer to an object?

```
Point blank = new Point(3, 4);
blank = null;
```

The first line creates a new `Point` object and makes `blank` refer to it. The second line changes `blank` so that instead of referring to the object, it refers to nothing. In the state diagram, we remove the arrow between them, as in Figure 10-7.

If there are no references to an object, there is no way to access its attributes or invoke a method on it. From the programmer's view, it ceases to exist. However it's still present in the computer's memory, taking up space.

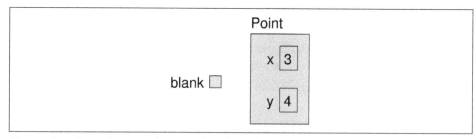

Figure 10-7. State diagram showing the effect of setting a variable to null.

As your program runs, the system automatically looks for stranded objects and reclaims them; then the space can be reused for new objects. This process is called **garbage collection**.

You don't have to do anything to make garbage collection happen, and in general don't have to be aware of it. But in high-performance applications, you may notice a slight delay every now and then when Java reclaims space from discarded objects.

Class Diagrams

To summarize what we've learned so far, Point and Rectangle objects each have their own attributes and methods. Attributes are an object's *data*, and methods are an object's *code*. An object's class defines which attributes and methods it will have.

In practice, it's more convenient to look at high-level pictures than to examine the source code. **Unified Modeling Language** (UML) defines a standard way to summarize the design of a class.

As shown in Figure 10-8, a **class diagram** is divided into two sections. The top half lists the attributes, and the bottom half lists the methods. UML uses a language-independent format, so rather than showing int x, the diagram uses x: int.

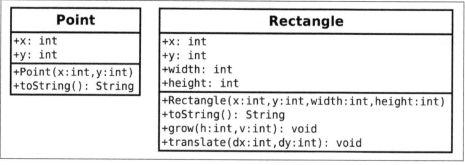

Figure 10-8. UML class diagrams for Point *and* Rectangle.

In contrast to state diagrams, which visualize objects (and variables) at run-time, a class diagram visualizes the source code at compile-time.

Both `Point` and `Rectangle` have additional methods; we are only showing the ones introduced in this chapter. See the documentation for these classes to learn more about what they can do.

Java Library Source

Throughout the book, you have used classes from the Java library including `System`, `String`, `Scanner`, `Math`, `Random`, and others. You may not have realized that these classes are written in Java. In fact, you can take a look at the source code to see how they work.

The Java library contains thousands of files, many of which are thousands of lines of code. That's more than one person could read and understand fully, so please don't be intimidated!

Because it's so large, the library source code is stored in a file named `src.zip`. Take a few minutes to locate this file on your machine:

- On Linux, it's likely under: `/usr/lib/jvm/openjdk-8/` (You might need to install the `openjdk-8-source` package.)
- On OS X, it's likely under: `/Library/Java/JavaVirtualMachines/jdk.../Contents/Home/`
- On Windows, it's likely under: `C:\Program Files\Java\jdk...\`

When you open (or unzip) the file, you will see folders that correspond to Java packages. For example, open the `java` folder and then open the `awt` folder. You should now see `Point.java` and `Rectangle.java`, along with the other classes in the `java.awt` package.

Open `Point.java` in your editor and skim through the file. It uses language features we haven't yet discussed, so you probably won't understand everything. But you can get a sense of what professional Java software looks like by browsing through the library.

Notice how much of `Point.java` is documentation. Each method is thoroughly commented, including `@param`, `@return`, and other Javadoc tags. Javadoc reads these comments and generates documentation in HTML. You can see the results by reading the documentation for the `Point` class, which you can find by doing a web search for "Java Point".

Now take a look at Rectangle's `grow` and `translate` methods. There is more to them than you may have realized, but that doesn't limit your ability to use these methods in a program.

To summarize the whole chapter, objects encapsulate data and provide methods to access and modify the data directly. Object-oriented programming makes it possible to hide messy details so that you can more easily use and understand code that other people wrote.

Vocabulary

attribute:
One of the named data items that make up an object.

dot notation:
Use of the dot operator (`.`) to access an object's attributes or methods.

object-oriented:
A way of organizing code and data into objects, rather than independent methods.

garbage collection:
The process of finding objects that have no references and reclaiming their storage space.

UML:
Unified Modeling Language, a standard way to draw diagrams for software engineering.

class diagram:
An illustration of the attributes and methods for a class.

Exercises

The code for this chapter is in the `ch10` directory of `ThinkJavaCode`. See "Using the Code Examples" on page xi for instructions on how to download the repository. Before you start the exercises, we recommend that you compile and run the examples.

Exercise 10-1.

The point of this exercise is to make sure you understand the mechanism for passing objects as parameters.

1. For the following program, draw a stack diagram showing the local variables and parameters of main and riddle just before riddle returns. Use arrows to show which objects each variable references.

2. What is the output of the program?

3. Is the blank object mutable or immutable? How can you tell?

```
public static int riddle(int x, Point p) {
    x = x + 7;
    return x + p.x + p.y;
}
public static void main(String[] args) {
    int x = 5;
    Point blank = new Point(1, 2);

    System.out.println(riddle(x, blank));
    System.out.println(x);
    System.out.println(blank.x);
    System.out.println(blank.y);
}
```

Exercise 10-2.

The point of this exercise is to make sure you understand the mechanism for returning new objects from methods.

1. Draw a stack diagram showing the state of the program just before distance returns. Include all variables and parameters, and show the objects those variables refer to.

2. What is the output of this program? (Can you tell without running it?)

```
public static double distance(Point p1, Point p2) {
    int dx = p2.x - p1.x;
    int dy = p2.y - p1.y;
    return Math.sqrt(dx * dx + dy * dy);
}

public static Point findCenter(Rectangle box) {
    int x = box.x + box.width / 2;
    int y = box.y + box.height / 2;
    return new Point(x, y);
}
```

```
public static void main(String[] args) {
    Point blank = new Point(5, 8);

    Rectangle rect = new Rectangle(0, 2, 4, 4);
    Point center = findCenter(rect);

    double dist = distance(center, blank);
    System.out.println(dist);
}
```

Exercise 10-3.

This exercise is about aliasing. Recall that aliases are two variables that refer to the same object.

1. Draw a diagram that shows the state of the program just before the end of main. Include all local variables and the objects they refer to.

2. What is the output of the program?

3. At the end of main, are p1 and p2 aliased? Why or why not?

```
public static void printPoint(Point p) {
    System.out.println("(" + p.x + ", " + p.y + ")");
}

public static Point findCenter(Rectangle box) {
    int x = box.x + box.width / 2;
    int y = box.y + box.height / 2;
    return new Point(x, y);
}

public static void main(String[] args) {
    Rectangle box1 = new Rectangle(2, 4, 7, 9);
    Point p1 = findCenter(box1);
    printPoint(p1);

    box1.grow(1, 1);
    Point p2 = findCenter(box1);
    printPoint(p2);
}
```

Exercise 10-4.

You might be sick of the factorial method by now, but we're going to do one more version.

1. Create a new program called Big.java and write (or reuse) an iterative version of factorial.

2. Display a table of the integers from 0 to 30 along with their factorials. At some point around 15, you will probably see that the answers are not right anymore. Why not?

3. BigInteger is a Java class that can represent arbitrarily big integers. There is no upper bound except the limitations of memory size and processing speed. Take a minute to read the documentation, which you can find by doing a web search for "Java BigInteger".

4. To use BigIntegers, you have to import java.math.BigInteger at the beginning of your program.

5. There are several ways to create a BigInteger, but the simplest uses valueOf. The following code converts an integer to a BigInteger:

```
int x = 17;
BigInteger big = BigInteger.valueOf(x);
```

6. Since BigIntegers are not primitive types, the usual math operators don't work. Instead, we have to use methods like add. To add two BigIntegers, invoke add on one and pass the other as an argument.

```
BigInteger small = BigInteger.valueOf(17);
BigInteger big = BigInteger.valueOf(1700000000);
BigInteger total = small.add(big);
```

Try out some of the other methods, like multiply and pow.

7. Convert factorial so that it performs its calculation using BigIntegers and returns a BigInteger as a result. You can leave the parameter alone; it will still be an integer.

8. Try displaying the table again with your modified factorial method. Is it correct up to 30? How high can you make it go?

9. Are BigInteger objects mutable or immutable? How can you tell?

Exercise 10-5.

Many encryption algorithms depend on the ability to raise large integers to a power. Here is a method that implements an efficient algorithm for integer exponentiation:

```
public static int pow(int x, int n) {
    if (n == 0) return 1;

    // find x to the n/2 recursively
    int t = pow(x, n / 2);

    // if n is even, the result is t squared
    // if n is odd, the result is t squared times x
    if (n % 2 == 0) {
        return t * t;
    } else {
        return t * t * x;
    }
}
```

The problem with this method is that it only works if the result is small enough to be represented by an int. Rewrite it so that the result is a BigInteger. The parameters should still be integers, though.

You should use the BigInteger methods add and multiply. But don't use BigInteger.pow; that would spoil the fun.

CHAPTER 11

Classes

Whenever you define a new class, you also create a new type with the same name. So way back in "The Hello World Program" on page 4, when we defined the class Hello, we created a type named Hello. We didn't declare any variables with type Hello, and we didn't use new to create a Hello object. It wouldn't have done much if we had—but we could have!

In this chapter, we will define classes that represent *useful* object types. We will also clarify the difference between classes and objects. Here are the most important ideas:

- Defining a **class** creates a new object type with the same name.
- Every object belongs to some object type; that is, it is an **instance** of some class.
- A class definition is like a template for objects: it specifies what attributes the objects have and what methods can operate on them.
- The new operator **instantiates** objects, that is, it creates new instances of a class.
- Think of a class like a blueprint for a house: you can use the same blueprint to build any number of houses.
- The methods that operate on an object type are defined in the class for that object.

The Time Class

One common reason to define a new class is to encapsulate related data in an object that can be treated as a single unit. That way, we can use objects as parameters and return values, rather than passing and returning multiple values. This design principle is called **data encapsulation**.

We have already seen two types that encapsulate data in this way: Point and Rectangle. Another example, which we will implement ourselves, is Time, which represents a time of day. The data encapsulated in a Time object are an hour, a minute, and a number of seconds. Because every Time object contains these data, we define attributes to hold them.

Attributes are also called **instance variables**, because each instance has its own variables (as opposed to class variables, coming up in "Class Variables" on page 164).

The first step is to decide what type each variable should be. It seems clear that hour and minute should be integers. Just to keep things interesting, let's make second a double.

Instance variables are declared at the beginning of the class definition, outside of any method. By itself, this code fragment is a legal class definition:

```
public class Time {
    private int hour;
    private int minute;
    private double second;
}
```

The Time class is public, which means that it can be used in other classes. But the instance variables are private, which means they can only be accessed from inside the Time class. If you try to read or write them from another class, you will get a compiler error.

Private instance variables help keep classes isolated from each other so that changes in one class won't require changes in other classes. It also simplifies what other programmers need to understand in order to use your classes. This kind of isolation is called **information hiding**.

Constructors

After declaring the instance variables, the next step is to define a **constructor**, which is a special method that initializes the instance variables. The syntax for constructors is similar to that of other methods, except:

- The name of the constructor is the same as the name of the class.
- Constructors have no return type (and no return value).
- The keyword static is omitted.

Here is an example constructor for the `Time` class:

```java
public Time() {
    this.hour = 0;
    this.minute = 0;
    this.second = 0.0;
}
```

This constructor does not take any arguments. Each line initializes an instance variable to zero (which in this example means midnight).

The name `this` is a keyword that refers to the object we are creating. You can use `this` the same way you use the name of any other object. For example, you can read and write the instance variables of `this`, and you can pass `this` as an argument to other methods. But you do not declare `this`, and you can't make an assignment to it.

A common error when writing constructors is to put a `return` statement at the end. Like void methods, constructors do not return values.

To create a `Time` object, you must use the new operator:

```java
Time time = new Time();
```

When you invoke `new`, Java creates the object and calls your constructor to initialize the instance variables. When the constructor is done, `new` returns a reference to the new object. In this example, the reference gets assigned to the variable `time`, which has type `Time`. Figure 11-1 shows the result.

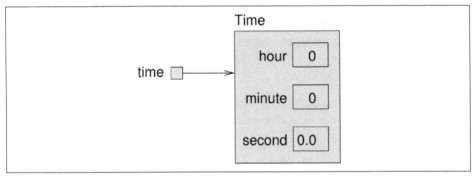

Figure 11-1. State diagram of a Time object.

Beginners sometimes make the mistake of invoking new inside the constructor. You don't have to, and you shouldn't. In this example, invoking `new Time()` in the constructor causes an infinite recursion:

```java
public Time() {
    new Time();        // wrong!
    this.hour = 0;
    this.minute = 0;
    this.second = 0.0;
}
```

More Constructors

Like other methods, constructors can be overloaded, which means you can provide multiple constructors with different parameters. Java knows which constructor to invoke by matching the arguments you provide with the parameters of the constructors.

It is common to provide a constructor that takes no arguments, like the previous one, and a "value constructor", like this one:

```java
public Time(int hour, int minute, double second) {
    this.hour = hour;
    this.minute = minute;
    this.second = second;
}
```

All this constructor does is copy values from the parameters to the instance variables. In this example, the names and types of the parameters are the same as the instance variables. As a result, the parameters **shadow** (or hide) the instance variables, so the keyword `this` is necessary to tell them apart. Parameters don't have to use the same names, but that's a common style.

To invoke this second constructor, you have to provide arguments after the new operator. This example creates a `Time` object that represents a fraction of a second before noon:

```java
Time time = new Time(11, 59, 59.9);
```

Overloading constructors provides the flexibility to create an object first and then fill in the attributes, or collect all the information before creating the object itself.

Once you get the hang of it, writing constructors gets boring. You can write them quickly just by looking at the list of instance variables. In fact, some IDEs can generate them for you.

Pulling it all together, here is the complete class definition so far:

```
public class Time {
    private int hour;
    private int minute;
    private double second;

    public Time() {
        this.hour = 0;
        this.minute = 0;
        this.second = 0.0;
    }

    public Time(int hour, int minute, double second) {
        this.hour = hour;
        this.minute = minute;
        this.second = second;
    }
}
```

Getters and Setters

Recall that the instance variables of Time are private. We can access them from within the Time class, but if we try to access them from another class, the compiler generates an error.

For example, here's a new class called TimeClient, because a class that uses objects defined in another class is called a **client**:

```
public class TimeClient {

    public static void main(String[] args) {
        Time time = new Time(11, 59, 59.9);
        System.out.println(time.hour);       // compiler error
    }
}
```

If you try to compile this code, you will get a message like hour has private access in Time. There are three ways to solve this problem:

- We could make the instance variables public.
- We could provide methods to access the instance variables.
- We could decide that it's not a problem, and refuse to let other classes access the instance variables.

The first choice is appealing because it's simple. But the problem is that when Class *A* accesses the instance variables of Class *B* directly, *A* becomes "dependent" on *B*. If anything in *B* changes later, it is likely that *A* will have to change, too.

But if *A* only uses methods to interact with *B*, *A* and *B* are "independent", which means that we can make changes in *B* without affecting *A* (as long as we don't change the method signatures).

So if we decide that `TimeClient` should be able to read the instance variables of `Time`, we can provide methods to do it:

```
public int getHour() {
    return this.hour;
}

public int getMinute() {
    return this.minute;
}

public int getSecond() {
    return this.second;
}
```

Methods like these are formally called "accessors", but more commonly referred to as **getters**. By convention, the method that gets a variable named `something` is called `getSomething`.

If we decide that `TimeClient` should also be able to modify the instance variables of `Time`, we can provide methods to do that, too:

```
public void setHour(int hour) {
    this.hour = hour;
}

public void setMinute(int minute) {
    this.minute = minute;
}

public void setSecond(int second) {
    this.second = second;
}
```

These methods are formally called "mutators", but more commonly known as **setters**. The naming convention is similar; the method that sets `something` is usually called `setSomething`.

Writing getters and setters can get boring, but many IDEs can generate them for you based on the instance variables.

Displaying Objects

If you create a `Time` object and display it with `println`:

```
public static void main(String[] args) {
    Time time = new Time(11, 59, 59.9);
    System.out.println(time);
}
```

The output will look something like:

```
Time@80cc7c0
```

When Java displays the value of an object type, it displays the name of the type and the address of the object (in hexadecimal). This address can be useful for debugging, if you want to keep track of individual objects.

To display `Time` objects in a way that is more meaningful to users, you could write a method to display the hour, minute, and second. Using `printTime` in "Multiple Parameters" on page 49 as a starting point, we could write:

```
public static void printTime(Time t) {
    System.out.print(t.hour);
    System.out.print(":");
    System.out.println(t.minute);
    System.out.print(":");
    System.out.println(t.second);
}
```

The output of this method, given the `time` object from the previous section, would be `11:59:59.9`. We can use `printf` to write it more concisely:

```
public static void printTime(Time t) {
    System.out.printf("%02d:%02d:%04.1f\n",
        t.hour, t.minute, t.second);
}
```

As a reminder, you need to use `%d` with integers and `%f` with floating-point numbers. The `02` option means "total width 2, with leading zeros if necessary", and the `04.1` option means "total width 4, one digit after the decimal point, leading zeros if necessary".

The toString Method

Every object type has a method called `toString` that returns a string representation of the object. When you display an object using `print` or `println`, Java invokes the object's `toString` method.

By default it simply displays the type of the object and its address, but you can **override** this behavior by providing your own `toString` method. For example, here is a `toString` method for `Time`:

```
public String toString() {
    return String.format("%02d:%02d:%04.1f\n",
        this.hour, this.minute, this.second);
}
```

The definition does not have the keyword `static`, because it is not a static method. It is an **instance method**, so called because when you invoke it, you invoke it on an instance of the class (`Time` in this case). Instance methods are sometimes called "non-static"; you might see this term in an error message.

The body of the method is similar to `printTime` in the previous section, with two changes:

- Inside the method, we use `this` to refer to the current instance; that is, the object the method is invoked on.
- Instead of `printf`, it uses `String.format`, which returns a formatted `String` rather than displaying it.

Now you can call `toString` directly:

```
Time time = new Time(11, 59, 59.9);
String s = time.toString();
```

Or you can invoke it indirectly through `println`:

```
System.out.println(time);
```

In this example, `this` in `toString` refers to the same object as `time`. The output is `11:59:59.9`.

The equals Method

We have seen two ways to check whether values are equal: the `==` operator and the `equals` method. With objects you can use either one, but they are not the same.

- The `==` operator checks whether objects are **identical**; that is, whether they are the same object.

  The `equals` method checks whether they are **equivalent**; that is, whether they have the same value.

The definition of identity is always the same, so the `==` operator always does the same thing. But the definition of equivalence is different for different objects, so objects can define their own `equals` methods.

Consider the following variables:

```
Time time1 = new Time(9, 30, 0.0);
Time time2 = time1;
Time time3 = new Time(9, 30, 0.0);
```

Figure 11-2 is a state diagram that shows these variables and their values.

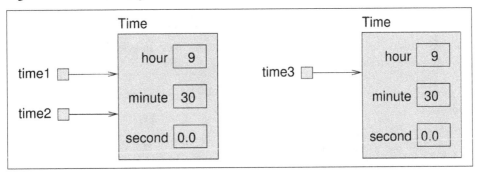

Figure 11-2. State diagram of three Time variables.

The assignment operator copies references, so time1 and time2 refer to the same object. Because they are identical, time1 == time2 is true.

But time1 and time3 refer to different objects. Because they are not identical, time1 == time3 is false.

By default, the equals method does the same thing as ==. For Time objects, that's probably not what we want. For example, time1 and time3 represent the same time of day, so we should consider them equivalent.

We can provide an equals method that implements this notion of equivalence:

```
public boolean equals(Time that) {
    return this.hour == that.hour
        && this.minute == that.minute
        && this.second == that.second;
}
```

equals is an instance method, so it uses this to refer to the current object and it doesn't have the keyword static. We can invoke equals as follows:

```
time1.equals(time3);
```

Inside the equals method, this refers to the same object as time1, and that refers to the same object as time3. Since their instance variables are equal, the result is true.

Many objects use a similar notion of equivalence; that is, two objects are equivalent if their instance variables are equal. But other definitions are possible.

Adding Times

Suppose you are going to a movie that starts at 18:50 (or 6:50 PM), and the running time is 2 hours 16 minutes. What time does the movie end?

We'll use `Time` objects to figure it out. Here are two ways we could "add" `Time` objects:

- We could write a static method that takes the two `Time` objects as parameters.
- We could write an instance method that gets invoked on one object and takes the other as a parameter.

To demonstrate the difference, we'll do both. Here is a rough draft that uses the static approach:

```java
public static Time add(Time t1, Time t2) {
    Time sum = new Time();
    sum.hour = t1.hour + t2.hour;
    sum.minute = t1.minute + t2.minute;
    sum.second = t1.second + t2.second;
    return sum;
}
```

And here's how we would invoke the static method:

```java
Time startTime = new Time(18, 50, 0.0);
Time runningTime = new Time(2, 16, 0.0);
Time endTime = Time.add(startTime, runningTime);
```

On the other hand, here's what it looks like as an instance method:

```java
public Time add(Time t2) {
    Time sum = new Time();
    sum.hour = this.hour + t2.hour;
    sum.minute = this.minute + t2.minute;
    sum.second = this.second + t2.second;
    return sum;
}
```

The changes are:

- We removed the keyword `static`.
- We removed the first parameter.
- We replaced `t1` with `this`.

Optionally, you could replace `t2` with `that`. Unlike `this`, `that` is not a keyword; it's just a slightly clever variable name.

And here's how we would invoke the instance method:

```java
Time endTime = startTime.add(runningTime);
```

That's all there is to it. Static methods and instance methods do the same thing, and you can convert from one to the other with just a few changes.

There's only one problem: the addition code itself is not correct. For this example, it returns 20:66, which is not a valid time. If second exceeds 59, we have to "carry" into the minutes column, and if minute exceeds 59, we have to carry into hour.

Here is a better version of add:

```java
public Time add(Time t2) {
    Time sum = new Time();
    sum.hour = this.hour + t2.hour;
    sum.minute = this.minute + t2.minute;
    sum.second = this.second + t2.second;

    if (sum.second >= 60.0) {
        sum.second -= 60.0;
        sum.minute += 1;
    }
    if (sum.minute >= 60) {
        sum.minute -= 60;
        sum.hour += 1;
    }
    return sum;
}
```

It's still possible that hour may exceed 23, but there's no days attribute to carry into. In that case, sum.hour -= 24 would yield the correct result.

Pure Methods and Modifiers

This implementation of add does not modify either of the parameters. Instead, it creates and returns a new Time object. As an alternative, we could have written a method like this:

```java
public void increment(double seconds) {
    this.second += seconds;
    while (this.second >= 60.0) {
        this.second -= 60.0;
        this.minute += 1;
    }
    while (this.minute >= 60) {
        this.minute -= 60;
        this.hour += 1;
    }
}
```

The increment method modifies an existing Time object. It doesn't create a new one, and it doesn't return anything.

In contrast, methods like add are called **pure** because:

- They don't modify the parameters.
- They don't have any other "side effects", like printing.
- The return value only depends on the parameters, not on any other state.

Methods like `increment`, which breaks the first rule, are sometimes called **modifiers**. They are usually void methods, but sometimes they return a reference to the object they modify.

Modifiers can be more efficient because they don't create new objects. But they can also be error-prone. When objects are aliased, the effects of modifiers can be confusing.

To make a class immutable, like `String`, you can provide getters but no setters and pure methods but no modifiers. Immutable objects can be more difficult to work with, at first, but they can save you from long hours of debugging.

Vocabulary

class:
> Previously, we defined a class as a collection of related methods. Now you know that a class is also a template for a new type of object.

instance:
> A member of a class. Every object is an instance of some class.

instantiate:
> Create a new instance of a class in the computer's memory.

data encapsulation:
> A technique for bundling multiple named variables into a single object.

instance variable:
> An attribute of an object; a non-static variable defined at the class level.

information hiding:
> The practice of making instance variables `private` to limit dependencies between classes.

constructor:
> A special method that initializes the instance variables of a newly-constructed object.

shadowing:
> Defining a local variable or parameter with the same name and type as an instance variable.

client:
> A class that uses objects defined in another class.

getter:
> A method that returns the value of an instance variable.

setter:
> A method that assigns a value to an instance variable.

override:
> Replacing a default implementation of a method, such as toString.

instance method:
> A non-static method that has access to this and the instance variables.

identical:
> Two values that are the same; in the case of objects, two variables that refer to the same object.

equivalent:
> Two objects that are "equal" but not necessarily identical, as defined by the equals method.

pure method:
> A static method that depends only on its parameters and no other data.

modifier method:
> A method that changes the state (instance variables) of an object.

Exercises

The code for this chapter is in the ch11 directory of ThinkJavaCode. See "Using the Code Examples" on page xi for instructions on how to download the repository. Before you start the exercises, we recommend that you compile and run the examples.

At this point you know enough to read Appendix B, which is about simple 2D graphics and animations. During the next few chapters, you should take a detour to read this appendix and work through the exercises.

Exercise 11-1.

Review the documentation of java.awt.Rectangle. Which methods are pure? Which are modifiers?

If you review the documentation of java.lang.String, you should see that there are no modifiers, because strings are immutable.

Exercise 11-2.

The implementation of increment in this chapter is not very efficient. Can you rewrite it so it doesn't use any loops? *Hint:* Remember the modulus operator.

Exercise 11-3.

In the board game Scrabble, each tile contains a letter, which is used to spell words in rows and columns, and a score, which is used to determine the value of words.

1. Write a definition for a class named Tile that represents Scrabble tiles. The instance variables should include a character named letter and an integer named value.
2. Write a constructor that takes parameters named letter and value and initializes the instance variables.
3. Write a method named printTile that takes a Tile object as a parameter and displays the instance variables in a reader-friendly format.
4. Write a method named testTile that creates a Tile object with the letter Z and the value 10, and then uses printTile to display the state of the object.
5. Implement the toString and equals methods for a Tile.
6. Create getters and setters for each of the attributes.

The point of this exercise is to practice the mechanical part of creating a new class definition and code that tests it.

Exercise 11-4.

Write a class definition for Date, an object type that contains three integers: year, month, and day. This class should provide two constructors. The first should take no parameters and initialize a default date. The second should take parameters named year, month and day, and use them to initialize the instance variables.

Write a main method that creates a new Date object named birthday. The new object should contain your birth date. You can use either constructor.

Exercise 11-5.

A rational number is a number that can be represented as the ratio of two integers. For example, 2/3 is a rational number, and you can think of 7 as a rational number with an implicit 1 in the denominator.

1. Define a class called `Rational`. A `Rational` object should have two integer instance variables that store the numerator and denominator.

2. Write a constructor that takes no arguments and that sets the numerator to 0 and denominator to 1.

3. Write an instance method called `printRational` that displays a `Rational` in some reasonable format.

4. Write a `main` method that creates a new object with type `Rational`, sets its instance variables to some values, and displays the object.

5. At this stage, you have a minimal testable program. Test it and, if necessary, debug it.

6. Write a `toString` method for `Rational` and test it using `println`.

7. Write a second constructor that takes two arguments and uses them to initialize the instance variables.

8. Write an instance method called `negate` that reverses the sign of a rational number. This method should be a modifier, so it should be void. Add lines to `main` to test the new method.

9. Write an instance method called `invert` that inverts the number by swapping the numerator and denominator. It should be a modifier. Add lines to `main` to test the new method.

10. Write an instance method called `toDouble` that converts the rational number to a double (floating-point number) and returns the result. This method is a pure method; it does not modify the object. As always, test the new method.

11. Write an instance method named `reduce` that reduces a rational number to its lowest terms by finding the greatest common divisor (GCD) of the numerator and denominator and dividing through. This method should be a pure method; it should not modify the instance variables of the object on which it is invoked.

    Hint: Finding the GCD only takes a few lines of code. Search the web for "Euclidean algorithm".

12. Write an instance method called `add` that takes a `Rational` number as an argument, adds it to `this`, and returns a new `Rational` object.

    There are several ways to add fractions. You can use any one you want, but you should make sure that the result of the operation is reduced so that the numerator and denominator have no common divisor (other than 1).

The purpose of this exercise is to write a class definition that includes a variety of methods, including constructors, static methods, instance methods, modifiers, and pure methods.

CHAPTER 12

Arrays of Objects

In the remaining chapters, we will develop programs that work with playing cards and decks of cards. Here is an outline of the road ahead:

- In this chapter, we define a `Card` class and write methods that work with cards and arrays of cards.

- In "The Deck Class" on page 175, we create a `Deck` class that encapsulates an array of cards, and we write methods that operate on decks.

- In Chapter 14, we introduce inheritance as a way to create new classes that extend existing classes. We then use all these classes to implement the card game *Crazy Eights*.

The code for this chapter is in `Card.java`, which is in the directory `ch12` in the repository for this book. Instructions for downloading this code are in "Using the Code Examples" on page xi.

Card Objects

If you are unfamiliar with traditional playing cards, now would be a good time to get a deck or read through *https://en.wikipedia.org/wiki/Standard_52-card_deck*.

There are 52 cards in a standard deck. Each card belongs to one of four suits and one of 13 ranks. The suits are Spades, Hearts, Diamonds, and Clubs. The ranks are Ace, 2, 3, 4, 5, 6, 7, 8, 9, 10, Jack, Queen, and King.

If we want to define a class to represent a playing card, it is pretty obvious what the instance variables should be: `rank` and `suit`. It is not as obvious what types they should be. One possibility is a `String` containing things like `"Spade"` for suits and

"Queen" for ranks. A problem with this design is that it would not be easy to compare cards to see which had a higher rank or suit.

An alternative is to use integers to **encode** the ranks and suits. By "encode" we don't mean to encrypt or translate into a secret code. We mean "define a mapping between a sequence of numbers and the things we want to represent."

Here is a mapping for suits:

Clubs $\mapsto$ 0
Diamonds $\mapsto$ 1
Hearts $\mapsto$ 2
Spades $\mapsto$ 3

We use the mathematical symbol $\mapsto$ to make it clear that these mappings are not part of the program. They are part of the program design, but they never appear explicitly in the code.

Each of the numerical ranks (2 through 10) maps to the corresponding integer, and for face cards:

Ace $\mapsto$ 1
Jack $\mapsto$ 11
Queen $\mapsto$ 12
King $\mapsto$ 13

So far, the class definition for the Card type looks like this:

```java
public class Card {
    private int rank;
    private int suit;

    public Card(int rank, int suit) {
        this.rank = rank;
        this.suit = suit;
    }
}
```

The instance variables are private: we can access them from inside this class, but not from other classes.

The constructor takes a parameter for each instance variable. To create a Card object, we use the new operator:

```java
Card threeOfClubs = new Card(3, 0);
```

The result is a reference to a Card that represents the 3 of Clubs.

Card toString

When you create a new class, the first step is to declare the instance variables and write constructors. A good next step is to write toString, which is useful for debugging and incremental development.

To display Card objects in a way that humans can read easily, we need to map the integer codes onto words. A natural way to do that is with an array of Strings. We can create the array like this:

```
String[] suits = new String[4];
```

And then assign values to the elements:

```
suits[0] = "Clubs";
suits[1] = "Diamonds";
suits[2] = "Hearts";
suits[3] = "Spades";
```

Or we can create the array and initialize the elements at the same time, as we saw in "Displaying Arrays" on page 105:

```
String[] suits = {"Clubs", "Diamonds", "Hearts", "Spades"};
```

The state diagram in Figure 12-1 shows the result. Each element of the array is a reference to a String.

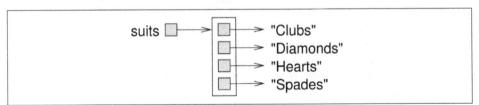

Figure 12-1. State diagram of an array of strings.

Now we need an array to decode the ranks:

```
String[] ranks = {null, "Ace", "2", "3", "4", "5", "6",
        "7", "8", "9", "10", "Jack", "Queen", "King"};
```

The zeroth element should never be used, because the only valid ranks are 1–13. We set it to null to indicate an unused element.

Using these arrays, we can create a meaningful String using suit and rank as indexes.

```
String s = ranks[card.rank] + " of " + suits[card.suit];
```

The expression suits[card.suit] means "use the instance variable suit from the object card as an index into the array suits."

Now we can wrap all that in a `toString` method.

```java
public String toString() {
    String[] ranks = {null, "Ace", "2", "3", "4", "5", "6",
                "7", "8", "9", "10", "Jack", "Queen", "King"};
    String[] suits = {"Clubs", "Diamonds", "Hearts", "Spades"};
    String s = ranks[this.rank] + " of " + suits[this.suit];
    return s;
}
```

When we display a card, `println` automatically calls `toString`:

```java
Card card = new Card(11, 1);
System.out.println(card);
```

The output is `Jack of Diamonds`.

Class Variables

So far we have seen local variables, which are declared inside a method, and instance variables, which are declared in a class definition, usually before the method definitions.

Local variables are created when a method is invoked, and their space is reclaimed when the method ends. Instance variables are created when you construct an object and reclaimed when the object is garbage-collected.

Now it's time to learn about **class variables**. Like instance variables, class variables are defined in a class definition, before the method definitions. But they are identified by the keyword `static`. They are created when the program begins (or when the class is used for the first time) and survive until the program ends. Class variables are *shared* across all instances of the class.

```java
public class Card {

    public static final String[] RANKS = {
        null, "Ace", "2", "3", "4", "5", "6", "7",
        "8", "9", "10", "Jack", "Queen", "King"};

    public static final String[] SUITS = {
        "Clubs", "Diamonds", "Hearts", "Spades"};

    // instance variables and constructors go here

    public String toString() {
        return RANKS[this.rank] + " of " + SUITS[this.suit];
    }
}
```

Class variables are often used to store constant values that are needed in several places. In that case, they should also be defined as `final`. Note that whether a variable is `static` or `final` involves two separate considerations: `static` means the variable is shared, and `final` means the variable is constant.

Naming `static final` variables with capital letters is a common convention that makes it easier to recognize their role in the class. Inside `toString` we can refer to `SUITS` and `RANKS` as if they were local variables, but we can tell that they are class variables.

One advantage of defining `SUITS` and `RANKS` as class variables is that they don't need to be created (and garbage-collected) every time `toString` is called. They may also be needed in other methods and classes, so it's helpful to make them available everywhere. Since the array variables are `final`, and the strings they reference are immutable, there is no danger in making them `public`.

The compareTo Method

As we saw in "The equals Method" on page 152, it's helpful to create an `equals` method to test whether two objects are equivalent.

```
public boolean equals(Card that) {
    return this.rank == that.rank
        && this.suit == that.suit;
}
```

It would also be nice to have a method for comparing cards, so we can tell if one is higher or lower than another. For primitive types, we can use the comparison operators—<, >, etc.—to compare values. But these operators don't work for object types.

For `Strings`, Java provides a `compareTo` method, as we saw in "String Comparison" on page 121. Like the `equals` method, we can write our own version of `compareTo` for the classes that we define.

Some types are "totally ordered", which means that you can compare any two values and tell which is bigger. Integers and strings are totally ordered.

Other types are "unordered", which means that there is no meaningful way to say that one element is bigger than another. In Java, the `boolean` type is unordered; if you try to compare `true < false`, you get a compiler error.

The set of playing cards is "partially ordered", which means that sometimes we can compare cards and sometimes not. For example, we know that the 3 of Clubs is higher than the 2 of Clubs, and the 3 of Diamonds is higher than the 3 of Clubs. But which is better, the 3 of Clubs or the 2 of Diamonds? One has a higher rank, but the other has a higher suit.

To make cards comparable, we have to decide which is more important: rank or suit. The choice is arbitrary, and it might be different for different games. But when you buy a new deck of cards, it comes sorted with all the Clubs together, followed by all the Diamonds, and so on. So for now, let's say that suit is more important.

With that decided, we can write `compareTo` as follows:

```java
public int compareTo(Card that) {
    if (this.suit < that.suit) {
        return -1;
    }
    if (this.suit > that.suit) {
        return 1;
    }
    if (this.rank < that.rank) {
        return -1;
    }
    if (this.rank > that.rank) {
        return 1;
    }
    return 0;
}
```

`compareTo` returns 1 if `this` wins, -1 if `that` wins, and 0 if they are equivalent. It compares suits first. If the suits are the same, it compares ranks. If the ranks are also the same, it returns 0.

Cards Are Immutable

The instance variables of `Card` are `private`, so they can't be accessed from other classes. We can provide getters to allow other classes to read the `rank` and `suit` values:

```java
public int getRank() {
    return this.rank;
}

public int getSuit() {
    return this.suit;
}
```

Whether or not to provide setters is a design decision. If we did, cards would be mutable, so you could transform one card into another. That is probably not a feature we need, and in general mutable objects are more error-prone. So it might be better to make cards immutable. To do that, all we have to do is *not* provide any modifier methods (including setters).

That's easy enough, but it is not foolproof, because some fool might come along later and add a modifier. We can prevent that possibility by declaring the instance variables final:

```
public class Card {
    private final int rank;
    private final int suit;

    ...
}
```

You can still assign values to these variables inside a constructor. But if someone writes a method that tries to modify these variables, they'll get a compiler error.

Arrays of Cards

Just as you can create an array of String objects, you can create an array of Card objects. The following statement creates an array of 52 cards:

```
Card[] cards = new Card[52];
```

Figure 12-2 shows the state diagram for this array.

Figure 12-2. State diagram of an unpopulated Card array.

Although we call it an "array of cards", the array contains *references* to objects; it does not contain the Card objects themselves. The elements are initialized to null. You can access the elements of the array in the usual way:

```
if (cards[0] == null) {
    System.out.println("No card yet!");
}
```

But if you try to access the instance variables of the non-existent Cards, you will get a NullPointerException.

```
cards[0].rank    // NullPointerException
```

That code won't work until we put cards in the array. One way to populate the array is to write nested for loops:

```
    int index = 0;
    for (int suit = 0; suit <= 3; suit++) {
        for (int rank = 1; rank <= 13; rank++) {
            cards[index] = new Card(rank, suit);
            index++;
        }
    }
```

The outer loop iterates suits from 0 to 3. For each suit, the inner loop iterates ranks from 1 to 13. Since the outer loop runs 4 times, and the inner loop runs 13 times for each suit, the body is executed 52 times.

We use a separate variable index to keep track of where in the array the next card should go. Figure 12-3 shows what the array looks like after the first two cards have been created.

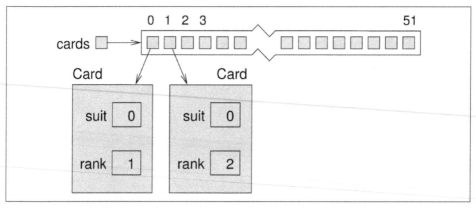

Figure 12-3. State diagram of a Card array with two cards.

When you work with arrays, it is convenient to have a method that displays the contents. We have seen the pattern for traversing an array several times, so the following method should be familiar:

```
public static void printDeck(Card[] cards) {
    for (int i = 0; i < cards.length; i++) {
        System.out.println(cards[i]);
    }
}
```

Since cards has type Card[], an element of cards has type Card. So println invokes the toString method in the Card class. This method is similar to invoking System.out.println(Arrays.toString(cards)).

Sequential Search

The next method we'll write is search, which takes an array of cards and a Card object as parameters. It returns the index where the Card appears in the array, or -1 if it doesn't. This version of search uses the algorithm we saw in "Array Traversal" on page 107, which is called **sequential search**:

```
public static int search(Card[] cards, Card target) {
    for (int i = 0; i < cards.length; i++) {
        if (cards[i].equals(target)) {
            return i;
        }
    }
    return -1;
}
```

The method returns as soon as it discovers the card, which means we don't have to traverse the entire array if we find the target. If we get to the end of the loop, we know the card is not in the array. Notice that this algorithm depends on the equals method.

If the cards in the array are not in order, there is no way to search faster than sequential search. We have to look at every card, because otherwise we can't be certain the card we want is not there. But if the cards are in order, we can use better algorithms.

We will learn in the next chapter how to sort arrays. If you pay the price to keep them sorted, finding elements becomes much easier. Especially for large arrays, sequential search is rather inefficient.

Binary Search

When you look for a word in a dictionary, you don't just search page by page from front to back. Since the words are in alphabetical order, you probably use a **binary search** algorithm:

1. Start on a page near the middle of the dictionary.

2. Compare a word on the page to the word you are looking for. If you find it, stop.

3. If the word on the page comes before the word you are looking for, flip to somewhere later in the dictionary and go to step 2.

4. If the word on the page comes after the word you are looking for, flip to somewhere earlier in the dictionary and go to step 2.

If you find two adjacent words on the page and your word comes between them, you can conclude that your word is not in the dictionary.

Getting back to the array of cards, we can write a faster version of search if we know the cards are in order:

```
public static int binarySearch(Card[] cards, Card target) {
    int low = 0;
    int high = cards.length - 1;
    while (low <= high) {
        int mid = (low + high) / 2;                    // step 1
        int comp = cards[mid].compareTo(target);

        if (comp == 0) {                               // step 2
            return mid;
        } else if (comp < 0) {                         // step 3
            low = mid + 1;
        } else {                                       // step 4
            high = mid - 1;
        }
    }
    return -1;
}
```

First, we declare low and high variables to represent the range we are searching. Initially we search the entire array, from 0 to length - 1.

Inside the while loop, we repeat the four steps of binary search:

1. Choose an index between low and high—call it mid—and compare the card at mid to the target.
2. If you found the target, return the index.
3. If the card at mid is lower than the target, search the range from mid + 1 to high.
4. If the card at mid is higher than the target, search the range from low to mid - 1.

If low exceeds high, there are no cards in the range, so we break out of the loop and return -1. Notice that this algorithm depends on the compareTo method of the object.

Tracing the Code

To see how binary search works, it's helpful to add the following print statement at the beginning of the loop:

```
System.out.println(low + ", " + high);
```

If we invoke binarySearch like this:

```
Card card = new Card(11, 0);
System.out.println(binarySearch(cards, card));
```

We expect to find this card at position 10. Here is the result:

```
0, 51
0, 24
0, 11
6, 11
9, 11
10
```

If we search for a card that's not in the array, like new Card(15, 1), which is the "15 of Diamonds", we get the following:

```
0, 51
26, 51
26, 37
26, 30
26, 27
-1
```

Each time through the loop, we cut the distance between low and high in half. After k iterations, the number of remaining cards is $52/2^k$. To find the number of iterations it takes to complete, we set $52/2^k = 1$ and solve for k. The result is $\log_2 52$, which is about 5.7. So we might have to look at 5 or 6 cards, as opposed to all 52 if we did a sequential search.

More generally, if the array contains n elements, binary search requires $\log_2 n$ comparisons, and sequential search requires n. For large values of n, binary search can be much faster.

Recursive Version

Another way to write a binary search is with a recursive method. The trick is to write a method that takes low and high as parameters, and turn steps 3 and 4 into recursive invocations. Here's what the code looks like:

```java
public static int binarySearch(Card[] cards, Card target,
                               int low, int high) {
    if (high < low) {
        return -1;
    }
    int mid = (low + high) / 2;                    // step 1
    int comp = cards[mid].compareTo(target);

    if (comp == 0) {                               // step 2
        return mid;
    } else if (comp < 0) {                         // step 3
        return binarySearch(cards, target, mid + 1, high);
    } else {                                       // step 4
        return binarySearch(cards, target, low, mid - 1);
    }
}
```

Instead of a `while` loop, we have an `if` statement to terminate the recursion. If `high` is less than `low`, there are no cards between them, and we conclude that the card is not in the array.

Two common errors in recursive programs are (1) forgetting to include a base case, and (2) writing the recursive call so that the base case is never reached. Either error causes infinite recursion and a `StackOverflowException`.

Vocabulary

encode:
> To represent one set of values using another set of values, by constructing a mapping between them.

class variable:
> A variable declared within a class as `static`. There is only one copy of a class variable, no matter how many objects there are.

sequential search:
> An algorithm that searches array elements, one by one, until a target value is found.

binary search:
> An algorithm that searches a sorted array by starting in the middle, comparing and element to the target, and eliminating half of the remaining elements.

Exercises

The code for this chapter is in the `ch12` directory of `ThinkJavaCode`. See "Using the Code Examples" on page xi for instructions on how to download the repository. Before you start the exercises, we recommend that you compile and run the examples.

Exercise 12-1.

Encapsulate the deck-building code from "Arrays of Cards" on page 167 in a method called `makeDeck` that takes no parameters and returns a fully-populated array of `Cards`.

Exercise 12-2.

In some card games, Aces are ranked higher than Kings. Modify the `compareTo` method to implement this ordering.

Exercise 12-3.

In Poker a "flush" is a hand that contains five or more cards of the same suit. A hand can contain any number of cards.

1. Write a method called `suitHist` that takes an array of cards as a parameter and that returns a histogram of the suits in the hand. Your solution should only traverse the array once.

2. Write a method called `hasFlush` that takes an array of cards as a parameter and returns `true` if the hand contains a flush (and `false` otherwise).

Exercise 12-4.

Working with cards is more interesting if you can display them on the screen. If you have not already read Appendix B about 2D graphics, you should read it before working on this exercise. In the code directory for this chapter, `ch12`, you will find:

- `cardset-oxymoron`: A directory containing images of playing cards.
- `CardTable.java`: A sample program that demonstrates how to read and display images.

This code demonstrates the use of a 2D array, specifically an array of images. The declaration looks like this:

```
private Image[][] images;
```

The variable `images` refers to a 2D array of `Image` objects, which are defined in the `java.awt` package. Here's the code that creates the array itself:

```
images = new Image[14][4];
```

The array has 14 rows (one for each rank plus an unused row for rank 0) and 4 columns (one for each suit). Here's the loop that populates the array:

```
String cardset = "cardset-oxymoron";
String suits = "cdhs";

for (int suit = 0; suit <= 3; suit++) {
    char c = suits.charAt(suit);

    for (int rank = 1; rank <= 13; rank++) {
        String s = String.format("%s/%02d%c.gif",
                                 cardset, rank, c);
        images[rank][suit] = new ImageIcon(s).getImage();
    }
}
```

The variable cardset contains the name of the directory that contains the image files. suits is a string that contains the single-letter abbreviations for the suits. These strings are used to assemble s, which contains the filename for each image. For example, when rank=1 and suit=2, the value of s is "cardset-oxymoron/01h.gif", which is an image of the Ace of Hearts.

The last line of the loop reads the image file, extracts an Image object, and assigns it to a location in the array, as specified by the indexes rank and suit. For example, the image of the Ace of Hearts is stored in row 1, column 2.

If you compile and run CardTable.java, you should see images of a deck of cards laid out on a green table. You can use this class as a starting place to implement your own card games.

CHAPTER 13

Objects of Arrays

In the previous chapter, we defined a class to represent cards and used an array of Card objects to represent a deck.

In this chapter, we take another step toward object-oriented programming by defining a class to represent a deck of cards. And we present algorithms for shuffling and sorting arrays.

The code for this chapter is in Card.java and Deck.java, which are in the directory ch13 in the repository for this book. Instructions for downloading this code are in "Using the Code Examples" on page xi.

The Deck Class

The main idea of this chapter is to create a Deck class that encapsulates an array of Cards. The initial class definition looks like this:

```java
public class Deck {
    private Card[] cards;

    public Deck(int n) {
        this.cards = new Card[n];
    }
}
```

The constructor initializes the instance variable with an array of n cards, but it doesn't create any card objects. Figure 13-1 shows what a Deck looks like with no cards.

Figure 13-1. State diagram of an unpopulated Deck object.

We'll add a second constructor that makes a standard 52-card deck and populates it with Card objects:

```
public Deck() {
    this.cards = new Card[52];
    int index = 0;
    for (int suit = 0; suit <= 3; suit++) {
        for (int rank = 1; rank <= 13; rank++) {
            this.cards[index] = new Card(rank, suit);
            index++;
        }
    }
}
```

This method is similar to the example in "Arrays of Cards" on page 167; we just turned it into a constructor. We can now create a standard Deck like this:

```
Deck deck = new Deck();
```

Now that we have a Deck class, we have a logical place to put methods that pertain to decks. Looking at the methods we have written so far, one obvious candidate is print Deck from "Arrays of Cards" on page 167.

```
public void print() {
    for (int i = 0; i < this.cards.length; i++) {
        System.out.println(this.cards[i]);
    }
}
```

When you transform a static method into an instance method, it usually gets shorter. We can simply type deck.print() to invoke the instance method.

Shuffling Decks

For most card games you need to be able to shuffle the deck; that is, put the cards in a random order. In "Random Numbers" on page 108 we saw how to generate random numbers, but it is not obvious how to use them to shuffle a deck.

One possibility is to model the way humans shuffle, which is usually dividing the deck in two halves and then choosing alternately from each one. Since humans usually don't shuffle perfectly, after about seven iterations the order of the deck is pretty well randomized.

But a computer program would have the annoying property of doing a perfect shuffle every time, which is not very random. In fact, after eight perfect shuffles, you would find the deck back in the order you started in! (For more information, see *https:// en.wikipedia.org/wiki/Faro_shuffle*.)

A better shuffling algorithm is to traverse the deck one card at a time, and at each iteration choose two cards and swap them. Here is an outline of how this algorithm works. To sketch the program, we will use a combination of Java statements and English. This technique is sometimes called **pseudocode**.

```
for each index i {
    // choose a random number between i and length - 1
    // swap the ith card and the randomly-chosen card
}
```

The nice thing about pseudocode is that it often makes clear what methods you are going to need. In this case, we need a method that chooses a random integer between `low` and `high`, and a method that takes two indexes and swaps the cards at those positions. Methods like these are called **helper methods**, because they help you implement more complex algorithms.

And this process—writing pseudocode first and then writing methods to make it work—is called **top-down development** (see *https://en.wikipedia.org/wiki/Top-down_and_bottom-up_design*).

One of the exercises at the end of the chapter asks you to write the helper methods `randomInt` and `swapCards` and use them to implement `shuffle`.

Selection Sort

Now that we have messed up the deck, we need a way to put it back in order. There is an algorithm for sorting that is ironically similar to the algorithm for shuffling. It's called **selection sort**, because it works by traversing the array repeatedly and selecting the lowest (or highest) remaining card each time.

During the first iteration, we find the lowest card and swap it with the card in the 0th position. During the *i*th iteration, we find the lowest card to the right of *i* and swap it with the *i*th card. Here is pseudocode for selection sort:

```
public void selectionSort() {
    for each index i {
        // find the lowest card at or to the right of i
        // swap the ith card and the lowest card found
    }
}
```

Again, the pseudocode helps with the design of the helper methods. In this algorithm we can use `swapCards` again, so we only need a method to find the lowest card; we'll call it `indexLowest`.

One of the exercises at the end of the chapter asks you to write the helper method `indexLowest` and use it to implement `selectionSort`.

Merge Sort

Selection sort is a simple algorithm, but it is not very efficient. To sort n items, it has to traverse the array $n - 1$ times. Each traversal takes an amount of time proportional to n. The total time, therefore, is proportional to n^2.

In the next two sections, we'll develop a more efficient algorithm called **merge sort**. To sort n items, merge sort takes time proportional to $n \log_2 n$. That may not seem impressive, but as n gets big, the difference between n^2 and $n \log_2 n$ can be enormous.

For example, $\log_2$ of one million is around 20. So if you had to sort a million numbers, selection sort would require one trillion steps; merge sort would require only 20 million.

The idea behind merge sort is this: if you have two subdecks, each of which has already been sorted, it is easy and fast to merge them into a single, sorted deck. Try this out with a deck of cards:

1. Form two subdecks with about 10 cards each, and sort them so that when they are face up the lowest cards are on top. Place both decks face up in front of you.

2. Compare the top card from each deck and choose the lower one. Flip it over and add it to the merged deck.

3. Repeat step 2 until one of the decks is empty. Then take the remaining cards and add them to the merged deck.

The result should be a single sorted deck. In the next few sections, we'll explain how to implement this algorithm in Java.

Subdecks

The first step of merge sort is to split the deck into two subdecks, each with about half the cards. So we might want a method, `subdeck`, that takes a deck and a range of indexes. It returns a new deck that contains the specified subset of the cards:

```
public Deck subdeck(int low, int high) {
    Deck sub = new Deck(high - low + 1);
    for (int i = 0; i < sub.cards.length; i++) {
        sub.cards[i] = this.cards[low + i];
    }
    return sub;
}
```

The first line creates an unpopulated subdeck. Inside the for loop, the subdeck gets populated with copies of references from the deck.

The length of the subdeck is high - low + 1, because both the low card and the high card are included. This sort of computation can be confusing, and forgetting the + 1 often leads to "off-by-one" errors. Drawing a picture is usually the best way to avoid them.

Figure 13-2 is a state diagram of a subdeck with low = 0 and high = 4. The result is a hand with five cards that are *shared* with the original deck; that is, they are aliased.

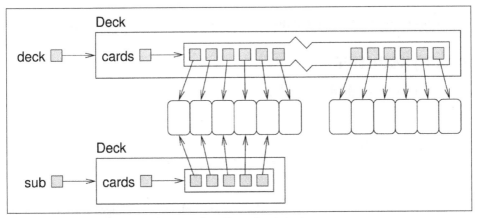

Figure 13-2. State diagram showing the effect of subdeck.

Aliasing might not be a good idea, because changes to shared cards would be reflected in multiple decks. But since Card objects are immutable, this kind of aliasing is not a problem at all.

Merging Decks

The next helper method we need is merge, which takes two sorted subdecks and returns a new deck containing all cards from both decks, in order. Here's what the algorithm looks like in pseudocode, assuming the subdecks are named d1 and d2:

```
public static Deck merge(Deck d1, Deck d2) {
    // create a new deck big enough for all the cards

    // use the index i to keep track of where we are at in
    // the first deck, and the index j for the second deck
    int i = 0;
    int j = 0;

    // the index k traverses the result deck
    for (int k = 0; k < result.cards.length; k++) {

        // if d1 is empty, d2 wins
        // if d2 is empty, d1 wins
        // otherwise, compare the two cards

        // add the winner to the new deck at position k
        // increment either i or j
    }
    // return the new deck
}
```

One of the exercises at the end of the chapter asks you to implement `merge`.

Adding Recursion

Once your `merge` method is working correctly, you can try out a simple version of merge sort:

```
public Deck almostMergeSort() {
    // divide the deck into two subdecks
    // sort the subdecks using selectionSort
    // merge the two halves and return the result
}
```

An exercise at the end of the chapter asks you to implement this algorithm. Once you get it working, the real fun begins! The magical thing about merge sort is that it is inherently recursive.

At the point where you sort the subdecks, why should you invoke the slower algorithm, `selectionSort`? Why not invoke the spiffy new `mergeSort` you are in the process of writing? Not only is that a good idea, it is *necessary* to achieve the $\log_2$ performance advantage.

To make `mergeSort` work recursively, you have to add a base case; otherwise it repeats forever. A simple base case is a subdeck with 0 or 1 cards. If `mergeSort` receives such a small subdeck, it can return it unmodified since it would already be sorted.

The recursive version of `mergeSort` should look something like this:

```
public Deck mergeSort() {
    // if the deck is 0 or 1 cards, return it
    // divide the deck into two subdecks
    // sort the subdecks using mergeSort
    // merge the two halves and return the result
}
```

As usual, there are two ways to think about recursive programs: you can think through the entire flow of execution, or you can make the "leap of faith" (see "Leap of Faith" on page 81). This example should encourage you to make the leap of faith.

When you used selectionSort to sort the subdecks, you didn't feel compelled to follow the flow of execution. You just assumed it works because you had already debugged it. And all you did to make mergeSort recursive was replace one sorting algorithm with another. There is no reason to read the program any differently.

Well, almost. You might have to give some thought to getting the base case right and making sure that you reach it eventually. But other than that, writing the recursive version should be no problem.

Vocabulary

pseudocode:
> A way of designing programs by writing rough drafts in a combination of English and Java.

helper method:
> Often a small method that does not do anything enormously useful by itself, but which helps another, more complex method.

top-down development:
> Breaking down a problem into sub-problems, and solving each sub-problem one at a time.

selection sort:
> A simple sorting algorithm that searches for the smallest or largest element n times.

merge sort:
> A recursive sorting algorithm that divides an array into two parts, sorts each part (using merge sort), and merges the results.

Exercises

The code for this chapter is in the ch13 directory of ThinkJavaCode. See "Using the Code Examples" on page xi for instructions on how to download the repository.

Before you start the exercises, we recommend that you compile and run the examples.

Exercise 13-1.

You can learn more about the sorting algorithms in this chapter, and others, at *http://www.sorting-algorithms.com/*. This site includes explanations of the algorithms, animations that show how they work, and analysis of their efficiency.

Exercise 13-2.

The goal of this exercise is to implement the shuffling algorithm from this chapter.

1. In the repository for this book, you should find a file called `Deck.java` that contains the code in this chapter. Check that you can compile it in your environment.

2. Add a `Deck` method called `randomInt` that takes two integers, `low` and `high`, and returns a random integer between `low` and `high`, including both. You can use the `nextInt` provided by `java.util.Random`, which we saw in "Random Numbers" on page 108. But you should avoid creating a `Random` object every time `randomInt` is invoked.

3. Write a method called `swapCards` that takes two indexes and swaps the cards at the given locations.

4. Write a method called `shuffle` that uses the algorithm in "Shuffling Decks" on page 176.

Exercise 13-3.

The goal of this exercise is to implement the sorting algorithms from this chapter. Use the `Deck.java` file from the previous exercise (or create a new one from scratch).

1. Write a method called `indexLowest` that uses the `compareCard` method to find the lowest card in a given range of the deck (from `lowIndex` to `highIndex`, including both).

2. Write a method called `selectionSort` that implements the selection sort algorithm in "Selection Sort" on page 177.

3. Using the pseudocode in "Merge Sort" on page 178, write the method called `merge`. The best way to test it is to build and shuffle a deck. Then use `subdeck` to form two small subdecks, and use selection sort to sort them. Then you can pass the two halves to `merge` to see if it works.

4. Write the simple version of mergeSort, the one that divides the deck in half, uses selectionSort to sort the two halves, and uses merge to create a new, sorted deck.

5. Write a recursive version of mergeSort. Remember that selectionSort is a modifier and mergeSort is a pure method, which means that they get invoked differently:

```
deck.selectionSort();      // modifies an existing deck
deck = deck.mergeSort();   // replaces old deck with new
```

Exercise 13-4.

The goal of this exercise is to practice top-down programming by implementing "insertion sort". Read about insertion sort at *http://www.sorting-algorithms.com/insertion-sort*. Write a method named insertionSort that implements this algorithm.

Exercise 13-5.

Write a toString method for the Deck class. It should return a single string that represents the cards in the deck. When it's printed, this string should display the same results as the print method in "The Deck Class" on page 175.

Hint: You can use the + operator to concatenate strings, but it is not very efficient. Consider using java.lang.StringBuilder; you can find the documentation by doing a web search for "Java StringBuilder".

CHAPTER 14

Objects of Objects

Now that we have classes that represent cards and decks, let's use them to make a game! *Crazy Eights* is a classic card game for two or more players. The main objective is to be the first player to get rid of all your cards. Here's how to play:

- Deal five or more cards to each player, and then deal one card face up to create the "discard pile". Place the remaining cards face down to create the "draw pile".

- Each player takes turns placing a single card on the discard pile. The card must match the rank or suit of the previously played card, or be an eight, which is a "wild card".

- When players don't have a matching card or an eight, they must draw new cards until they get one.

- If the draw pile ever runs out, the discard pile is shuffled (except the top card) and becomes the new draw pile.

- As soon as a player has no cards, the game ends and all other players score penalty points for their remaining cards. Eights are worth 20, face cards are worth 10, and all others are worth their rank.

You can read *https://en.wikipedia.org/wiki/Crazy_Eights* for more details, but we have enough to get started.

The code for this chapter is in the directory ch14 in the repository for this book. Instructions for downloading this code are in "Using the Code Examples" on page xi.

Decks and Hands

To implement this game, we need to represent a deck of cards, a discard pile, a draw pile, and a hand for each player. And we need to be able to deal, draw, and discard cards.

The `Deck` class from the previous chapter meets some of these requirements, but there are two problems:

- Hands and piles have different sizes, and their sizes change as the game progresses. Our implementation of `Deck` uses a `Card` array, and the size of an array can't change.

- It's not clear that a `Deck` object is the right way to represent hands and piles. We might want new classes for other collections of cards.

We can solve the first problem by replacing the `Card` array with an `ArrayList`, which is in the `java.util` package. An `ArrayList` is a **collection**, which is an object that contains other objects.

The Java library provides a variety of collections. For our purposes, `ArrayList` is a good choice because it provides methods to add and remove elements, and it grows and shrinks automatically.

To solve the second problem, we can use a language feature called **inheritance**. We'll define a new class, `CardCollection`, to represent a collection of cards. Then we'll define `Deck` and `Hand` as subclasses of `CardCollection`.

A **subclass** is a new class that "extends" an existing class; that is, it has the attributes and methods of the existing class, plus more. We'll see the details soon, but let's start with `CardCollection`:

CardCollection

Here's the beginning of a `CardCollection` class that uses `ArrayList` instead of a primitive array:

```java
public class CardCollection {

    private String label;
    private ArrayList<Card> cards;

    public CardCollection(String label) {
        this.label = label;
        this.cards = new ArrayList<Card>();
    }
}
```

When you declare an `ArrayList`, you specify the type it contains in angle brackets (`<>`). This declaration says that `cards` is not just an `ArrayList`, it's an `ArrayList` of `Card` objects.

The constructor takes a string as an argument and assigns it to an instance variable, `label`. It also initializes `cards` with an empty `ArrayList`.

`ArrayList` provides a method, `add`, that adds an element to the collection. We will write a `CardCollection` method that does the same thing:

```
public void addCard(Card card) {
    this.cards.add(card);
}
```

Until now, we have used `this` explicitly to make it easy to identify attributes. Inside `addCard` and other instance methods, you can access instance variables without using the keyword `this`. So from here on, we will drop it:

```
public void addCard(Card card) {
    cards.add(card);
}
```

We also need to be able to remove cards from a collection. The following method takes an index, removes the card at that location, and shifts the following cards left to fill the gap:

```
public Card popCard(int i) {
    return cards.remove(i);
}
```

If we are dealing cards from a shuffled deck, we don't care which card gets removed. It is most efficient to choose the last one, so we don't have to shift any following cards. Here is an overloaded version of `popCard` that removes and returns the last card:

```
public Card popCard() {
    int i = size() - 1;
    return popCard(i);
}
```

Notice that `popCard` uses `CardCollection`'s own `size` method, which in turn calls the `ArrayList`'s `size` method:

```
public int size() {
    return cards.size();
}
```

For convenience, `CardCollection` also provides an `empty` method that returns `true` when `size` is zero:

```
public boolean empty() {
    return cards.size() == 0;
}
```

Methods like addCard, popCard, and size, which invoke another method without doing much additional work, are called **wrapper methods**. We will use these wrapper methods to implement less trivial methods, like deal:

```
public void deal(CardCollection that, int n) {
    for (int i = 0; i < n; i++) {
        Card card = popCard();
        that.addCard(card);
    }
}
```

The deal method removes cards from the collection it is invoked on, this, and adds them to the collection it gets as a parameter, that. The second parameter, n, is the number of cards to deal.

To access the elements of an ArrayList, you can't use the array [] operator. Instead, you have to use the methods get and set. Here is a wrapper for get:

```
public Card getCard(int i) {
    return cards.get(i);
}
```

The last method gets the last card (but doesn't remove it):

```
public Card last() {
    int i = size() - 1;
    return cards.get(i);
}
```

In order to control the ways card collections are modified, we don't provide a wrapper for set. The only modifiers we provide are the two versions of popCard and the following version of swapCards:

```
public void swapCards(int i, int j) {
    Card temp = cards.get(i);
    cards.set(i, cards.get(j));
    cards.set(j, temp);
}
```

We use swapCards to implement shuffle, which we described in "Shuffling Decks" on page 176:

```
public void shuffle() {
    Random random = new Random();
    for (int i = size() - 1; i > 0; i--) {
        int j = random.nextInt(i);
        swapCards(i, j);
    }
}
```

ArrayList provides additional methods we aren't using here. You can read about them in the documentation, which you can find by doing a web search for "Java ArrayList".

Inheritance

At this point we have a class that represents a collection of cards. Next we'll use it to define Deck and Hand. Here is the complete definition of Deck:

```java
public class Deck extends CardCollection {

    public Deck(String label) {
        super(label);

        for (int suit = 0; suit <= 3; suit++) {
            for (int rank = 1; rank <= 13; rank++) {
                cards.add(new Card(rank, suit));
            }
        }
    }
}
```

The first line uses the keyword extends to indicate that Deck extends the class Card Collection. That means a Deck object has the same instance variables and methods as a CardCollection. Another way to say the same thing is that Deck "inherits from" CardCollection. We could also say that CardCollection is a **superclass**, and Deck is one of its subclasses.

In Java, classes may only extend one superclass. Classes that do not specify a superclass with extends automatically inherit from java.lang.Object. So in this example, Deck extends CardCollection, which in turn extends Object. The Object class provides the default equals and toString methods, among other things.

Constructors are not inherited, but all other public attributes and methods are. The only additional method in Deck, at least for now, is a constructor. So you can create a Deck object like this:

```java
Deck deck = new Deck("Deck");
```

The first line of the constructor uses something new, super, which is a keyword that refers to the superclass of the current class. When super is used like a method, as in this example, it invokes the constructor of the superclass.

So in this case, super invokes the CardCollection constructor, which initializes the attributes label and cards. When it returns, the Deck constructor resumes and populates the (empty) ArrayList with Card objects.

That's it for the Deck class. Next we need a way to represent a hand, which is the collection of cards held by a player, and a pile, which is a collection of cards on the table. We could define two classes, one for hands and one for piles, but there is not much difference between them. So we'll use one class, called Hand, for both hands and piles. Here's what the definition looks like:

```
public class Hand extends CardCollection {

    public Hand(String label) {
        super(label);
    }

    public void display() {
        System.out.println(getLabel() + ": ");
        for (int i = 0; i < size(); i++) {
            System.out.println(getCard(i));
        }
        System.out.println();
    }
}
```

Like Deck, Hand extends CardCollection, so it inherits methods like getLabel, size, and getCard, which are used in display. Hand also provides a constructor, which invokes the constructor of CardCollection (and nothing else).

In summary, a Deck is just like a CardCollection, but it provides a different constructor. And a Hand is just like a CardCollection, but it provides an additional method, display.

Dealing Cards

At this point we can create a Deck and start dealing cards. Here's a simple example that deals five cards to a hand, and deals the rest into a draw pile:

```
Deck deck = new Deck("Deck");
deck.shuffle();

Hand hand = new Hand("Hand");
deck.deal(hand, 5);
hand.display();

Hand drawPile = new Hand("Draw Pile");
deck.dealAll(drawPile);
System.out.printf("Draw Pile has %d cards.\n",
                  drawPile.size());
```

CardCollection provides dealAll, which deals all of the remaining cards. Here's the output of the previous example:

```
Hand:
5 of Diamonds
Ace of Hearts
6 of Clubs
6 of Diamonds
2 of Clubs

Draw Pile has 47 cards.
```

Of course, if you run this example you will probably get a different hand, because the deck is shuffled randomly.

If you are a careful reader, you might notice something strange about this example. Take another look at the definition of deal:

```
public void deal(CardCollection that, int n) {
    for (int i = 0; i < n; i++) {
        Card card = popCard();
        that.addCard(card);
    }
}
```

Notice that the first parameter is supposed to be a CardCollection. But we invoked it like this:

```
Hand hand = new Hand("Hand");
deck.deal(hand, 5);
```

The argument is a Hand, not a CardCollection. So why is this example legal? It's because Hand is a subclass of CardCollection, so a Hand object is also considered to be a CardCollection object. If a method expects a CardCollection, you can give it a Hand, a Deck, or a CardCollection.

But it doesn't work the other way around: not every CardCollection is a Hand, so if a method expects a Hand, you have to give it a Hand, not a CardCollection.

If it seems strange that an object can belong to more than one type, remember that this happens in real life, too. Every cat is also a mammal, and every mammal is also an animal. But not every animal is a mammal, and not every mammal is a cat.

The Player Class

The classes we have defined so far could be used for any card game; we have not yet implemented any of the rules specific to *Crazy Eights*. And that's probably a good thing, since it makes it easy to reuse these classes if we want to make another game in the future.

But now it's time to implement the rules. We'll use two classes: Player, which encapsulates player strategy, and Eights, which creates and maintains the state of the game. Here is the beginning of the Player definition:

```
public class Player {

    private String name;
    private Hand hand;

    public Player(String name) {
        this.name = name;
        this.hand = new Hand(name);
    }
```

A `Player` has two `private` attributes: a name and a hand. The constructor takes the player's name as a string and saves it in an instance variable. In this example, we have to use `this` to distinguish between the instance variable and the parameter with the same name.

The primary method that `Player` provides is `play`, which decides which card to discard during each turn:

```
public Card play(Eights eights, Card prev) {
    Card card = searchForMatch(prev);
    if (card == null) {
        card = drawForMatch(eights, prev);
    }
    return card;
}
```

The first parameter is a reference to the `Eights` object that encapsulates the state of the game. We'll need it if we have to draw a new card. The second parameter, `prev`, is the card on top of the discard pile.

Using top-down development, we'll have `play` invoke two helper methods, `searchForMatch` and `drawForMatch`. `searchForMatch` looks in the player's hand for a card that matches the previously played card:

```
public Card searchForMatch(Card prev) {
    for (int i = 0; i < hand.size(); i++) {
        Card card = hand.getCard(i);
        if (cardMatches(card, prev)) {
            return hand.popCard(i);
        }
    }
    return null;
}
```

The strategy is pretty simple: the for loop searches for the first card that's legal to play and returns it. If there are no cards that match, it returns `null`. And in that case, we have to draw cards until we get a match:

```
public Card drawForMatch(Eights eights, Card prev) {
    while (true) {
        Card card = eights.draw();
        System.out.println(name + " draws " + card);
        if (cardMatches(card, prev)) {
            return card;
        }
        hand.addCard(card);
    }
}
```

The while loop runs until it finds a match (we'll assume for now that it always does).
It uses the Eights object to draw a card. If it matches, it returns the card. Otherwise it
adds the card to the player's hand and continues.

Both searchForMatch and drawForMatch use cardMatches, which is a static method,
also defined in Player. cardMatches is a straightforward translation of the rules of
the game:

```
public static boolean cardMatches(Card card1, Card card2) {
    if (card1.getSuit() == card2.getSuit()) {
        return true;
    }
    if (card1.getRank() == card2.getRank()) {
        return true;
    }
    if (card1.getRank() == 8) {
        return true;
    }
    return false;
}
```

Finally, Player provides score, which computes penalty points for cards left in a
player's hand at the end of the game:

```
public int score() {
    int sum = 0;
    for (int i = 0; i < hand.size(); i++) {
        Card card = hand.getCard(i);
        int rank = card.getRank();
        if (rank == 8) {
            sum -= 20;
        } else if (rank > 10) {
            sum -= 10;
        } else {
            sum -= rank;
        }
    }
    return sum;
}
```

The Eights Class

In "Shuffling Decks" on page 176 we introduced top-down development, which is a way of developing programs by identifying high-level goals, like shuffling a deck, and breaking them into smaller problems, like finding the lowest element in an array or swapping two elements.

In this section we present **bottom-up development**, which goes the other way around: first we identify simple pieces we need, then we assemble them into more complex algorithms.

Looking at the rules of *Crazy Eights*, we can identify some methods we'll need:

- Create the deck, the discard and draw piles, and the player objects.
- Deal the cards.
- Check whether the game is over.
- If the draw pile is empty, shuffle the discard pile and move the cards into the draw pile.
- Draw a card.
- Keep track of whose turn it is and switch from one player to the next.
- Display the state of the game.
- Wait for the user before running the next turn.

Now we can start implementing the pieces. Here is the beginning of the class definition for Eights, which encapsulates the state of the game:

```
public class Eights {

    private Player one;
    private Player two;
    private Hand drawPile;
    private Hand discardPile;
    private Scanner in;
```

In this version, there are always two players. One of the exercises at the end of the chapter asks you to modify this code to handle more players.

The last instance variable is a Scanner that we'll use to prompt the user after each move. Here's a constructor that initializes the instance variables and deals the cards:

```
public Eights() {
    Deck deck = new Deck("Deck");
    deck.shuffle();

    int handSize = 5;
    one = new Player("Allen");
    deck.deal(one.getHand(), handSize);
```

```
two = new Player("Chris");
deck.deal(two.getHand(), handSize);

discardPile = new Hand("Discards");
deck.deal(discardPile, 1);

drawPile = new Hand("Draw pile");
deck.dealAll(drawPile);

in = new Scanner(System.in);
}
```

The next piece we'll need is a method that checks whether the game is over. If either hand is empty, we're done:

```
public boolean isDone() {
    return one.getHand().empty() || two.getHand().empty();
}
```

When the draw pile is empty, we have to shuffle the discard pile. Here is a method for that:

```
public void reshuffle() {
    Card prev = discardPile.popCard();
    discardPile.dealAll(drawPile);
    discardPile.addCard(prev);
    drawPile.shuffle();
}
```

The first line saves the top card from discardPile. The next line transfers the rest of the cards to drawPile. Then we put the saved card back into discardPile and shuffle drawPile.

Now we can use reshuffle as part of draw:

```
public Card draw() {
    if (drawPile.empty()) {
        reshuffle();
    }
    return drawPile.popCard();
}
```

We can switch from one player to the next like this:

```
public Player nextPlayer(Player current) {
    if (current == one) {
        return two;
    } else {
        return one;
    }
}
```

The nextPlayer method takes the current player as a parameter and returns the player who should go next.

The last two pieces are `displayState` and `waitForUser`:

```java
public void displayState() {
    one.display();
    two.display();
    discardPile.display();
    System.out.println("Draw pile:");
    System.out.println(drawPile.size() + " cards");
}

public void waitForUser() {
    in.nextLine();
}
```

Using these pieces, we can write `takeTurn`, which executes one player's turn:

```java
public void takeTurn(Player player) {
    Card prev = discardPile.last();
    Card next = player.play(this, prev);
    discardPile.addCard(next);

    System.out.println(player.getName() + " plays " + next);
    System.out.println();
}
```

`takeTurn` reads the top card off the discard pile and passes it to `player.play`, which we saw in the previous section. The result is the card the player chose, which is added to the discard pile.

Finally, we use `takeTurn` and the other methods to write `playGame`:

```java
public void playGame() {
    Player player = one;

    // keep playing until there's a winner
    while (!isDone()) {
        displayState();
        waitForUser();
        takeTurn(player);
        player = nextPlayer(player);
    }

    // display the final score
    one.displayScore();
    two.displayScore();
}
```

Done! Notice the result of bottom-up development is similar to top-down: we have a high-level method that calls helper methods. The main difference is the order we used to arrive at this solution.

Class Relationships

This chapter demonstrates two common relationships between classes:

composition:
> Instances of one class contain references to instances of another class. For example, an instance of Eights contains references to two Player objects, two Hand objects, and a Scanner.

inheritance:
> One class extends another class. For example, Hand extends CardCollection, so every instance of Hand is also a CardCollection.

Composition is also known as a **HAS-A** relationship, as in "Eights HAS-A Scanner". Inheritance is also known as an **IS-A** relationship, as in "a Hand IS-A CardCollection". This vocabulary provides a concise way to talk about an object-oriented design.

There is also a standard way to represent these relationships graphically in UML class diagrams. As we saw in "Class Diagrams" on page 138, the UML representation of a class is a box with three sections: the class name, the attributes, and the methods. The latter two sections are optional when showing relationships.

Relationships between classes are represented by arrows: composition arrows have a standard arrow head, and inheritance arrows have a hollow triangle head (usually pointing up). Figure 14-1 shows the classes defined in this chapter and the relationships among them.

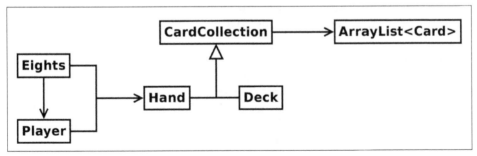

Figure 14-1. UML diagram for the classes in this chapter.

UML is an international standard, so almost any software engineer in the world could look at this diagram and understand our design. And class diagrams are only one of many graphical representations defined in the UML standard.

We hope this final chapter has been a useful summary of all the techniques presented in the book, including variables, methods, conditionals, loops, arrays, objects, and algorithms. Congratulations on making it to the end!

Vocabulary

collection:
An object that contains other objects, or more specifically, one of the objects in the Java library, like ArrayList, that contains objects.

inheritance:
The ability to define a new class that has the same instance variables and methods of an existing class.

subclass:
A class that inherits from, or extends, an existing class.

superclass:
An existing class that is extended by another class.

wrapper method:
A method that calls another method without doing much additional work.

bottom-up development:
A way of developing programs by identifying simple pieces, implementing them, and then assembling them into more complex algorithms.

HAS-A:
A relationship between two classes where one class "has" an instance of another class as one of its attributes.

IS-A:
A relationship between two classes where one class extends another class; the subclass "is" an instance of the superclass.

Exercises

The code for this chapter is in the ch14 directory of ThinkJavaCode. See "Using the Code Examples" on page xi for instructions on how to download the repository. Before you start the exercises, we recommend that you compile and run the examples.

Exercise 14-1.

Design a better strategy for the Player.play method. For example, if there are multiple cards you can play, and one of them is an eight, you might want to play the eight.

Think of other ways you can minimize penalty points, such as playing the highest ranking cards first. Write a new class that extends Player and overrides play to implement your strategy.

Exercise 14-2.

Write a loop that plays the game 100 times and keeps track of how many times each player wins. If you implemented multiple strategies in the previous exercise, you can play them against each other to evaluate which one works best.

Hint: Design a Genius class that extends Player and overrides the play method, and then replace one of the players with a Genius object.

Exercise 14-3.

One limitation of the program we wrote in this chapter is that it only handles two players. Modify the Eights class to create an ArrayList of players, and modify next Player to select the next player.

Exercise 14-4.

When we designed the program for this chapter, we tried to minimize the number of classes. As a result, we ended up with a few awkward methods. For example, card Matches is a static method in Player, but it would be more natural if it were an instance method in Card.

The problem is that Card is supposed to be useful for any card game, not just *Crazy Eights*. You can solve this problem by adding a new class, EightsCard, that extends Card and provides a method, match, that checks whether two cards match according to the rules of *Crazy Eights*.

At the same time, you could create a new class, EightsHand, that extends Hand and provides a method, scoreHand, that adds up the scores of the cards in the hand. And while you're at it, you could add a method named scoreCard to EightsCard.

Whether or not you actually make these changes, draw a UML class diagram that shows this alternative object hierarchy.

Development Tools

The steps for compiling, running, and debugging Java code depend on your development environment and operating system. We avoided putting these details in the main text, because they can be distracting. Instead, we provide this appendix with a brief introduction to DrJava—an **integrated development environment** (IDE) that is well suited for beginners—and other development tools, including Checkstyle for code quality and JUnit for testing.

Installing DrJava

The easiest way to start programming in Java is to use a website that compiles and runs Java code in the browser. Examples include *jdoodle.com*, *compilejava.net*, *tutorialspoint.com*, and others.

If you are unable to install software on your computer (which is often the case in public schools and Internet cafés), you can use these online development environments for almost everything in this book.

But if you want to compile and run Java programs on your own computer, you will need:

- The **Java Development Kit** (JDK), which includes the compiler, the **Java Virtual Machine** (JVM) that interprets the compiled byte code, and other tools such as Javadoc.
- A simple **text editor** such as Notepad++ or Sublime Text, and/or an IDE such as DrJava, Eclipse, jGrasp, or NetBeans.

The JDK we recommend is Java SE (Standard Edition), which Oracle makes available for free. The IDE we recommend is DrJava, which is an open-source development environment written in Java (see Figure A-1).

To install the JDK, search the web for "download JDK" which should take you to Oracle's website. Scroll down to "Java Platform, Standard Edition" and click the download button under JDK. Then accept the license agreement and select the installer for your operating system. Don't forget to run the installer after you download it!

To install DrJava, visit *http://drjava.org* and download the **JAR** file. We recommend that you save it to your Desktop or another convenient location. Simply double-click the JAR file to run DrJava. Refer to the DrJava documentation (*http://drjava.org/docs/quickstart/*) for more details.

Figure A-1. Screenshot of DrJava editing the hello world program.

When running DrJava for the first time, we recommend you change three settings from the *Edit > Preferences* menu under *Miscellaneous*: set the *Indent Level* to 4, check the *Automatically Close Block Comments* box, and uncheck the *Keep Emacs-style Backup Files* box.

DrJava Interactions

One of the most useful features of DrJava is the "Interactions Pane" at the bottom of the window. It provides the ability to try out code quickly, without having to write a class definition and save/compile/run the program. Figure A-2 shows an example.

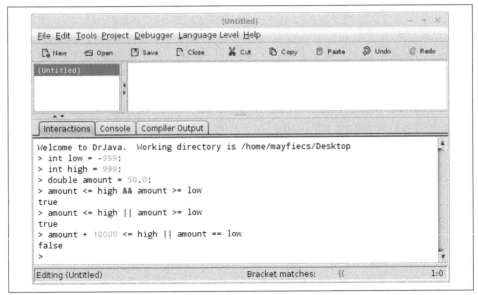

Figure A-2. Screenshot of the Interactions Pane in DrJava.

There is one subtle detail to note when using the Interactions feature. If you don't end an expression (or statement) with a semicolon, DrJava automatically displays its value. Notice in Figure A-2 how the variable declarations end with semicolons, but the logic expressions in the following lines do not. This feature saves you from having to type `System.out.println` every time.

What's nice about this feature is that you don't have to create a new class, declare a `main` method, write arbitrary expressions inside `System.out.println` statements, save the source file, and get all of your code to compile in advance. Also, you can press the up/down arrows on the keyboard to repeat previous commands and experiment with incremental differences.

Command-Line Interface

One of the most powerful and useful skills you can learn is how to use the **command-line interface**, also called the "terminal". The command line is a direct interface to the operating system. It allows you to run programs, manage files and directories, and monitor system resources. Many advanced tools, both for software development and general purpose computing, are available only at the command line.

There are many good tutorials online for learning the command line for your operating system; just search the web for "command line tutorial". On Unix systems like Linux and OS X, you can get started with just four commands: change the working directory (cd), list directory contents (ls), compile Java programs (javac), and run Java programs (java).

Figure A-3 shows an example where the Hello.java source file is stored in the Desktop directory. After changing to that location and listing the files, we use the javac command to compile Hello.java. Running ls again, we see that the compiler generated a new file, Hello.class, which contains the byte code. We run the program using the java command, which displays the output on the following line.

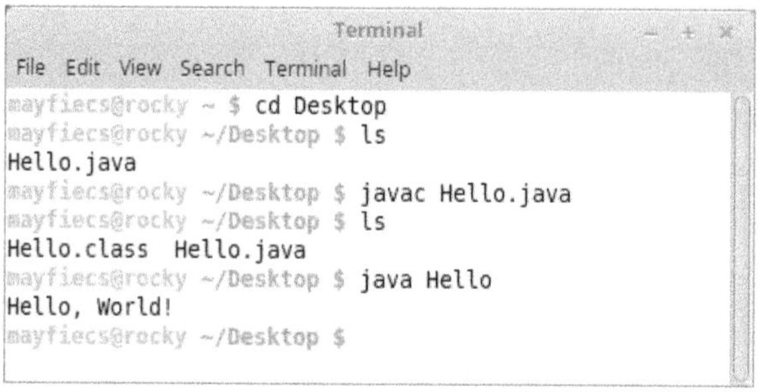

Figure A-3. Compiling and running Hello.java from the command line.

Note that the javac command requires a *filename* (or multiple source files separated by spaces), whereas the java command requires a single *class name*. If you use DrJava, it runs these commands for you behind the scenes and displays the output in the Interactions Pane.

Taking time to learn this efficient and elegant way of interacting with your operating system will make you more productive. People who don't use the command line don't know what they're missing.

Command-Line Testing

As described in "Debugging Code" on page 8, it's more effective to program and debug your code little by little than to attempt writing everything all at once. And after you've completed programming an algorithm, it's important to test that it works correctly on a variety of inputs.

Throughout the book, we illustrate techniques for testing your programs. Most if not all testing is based on a simple idea: does the program do what we expect it to do? For simple programs, it's not difficult to run them several times and see what happens. But at some point, you will get tired of typing the same test cases over and over.

We can automate the process of entering input and comparing "expected output" with "actual output" using the command line. The basic idea is to store the test cases in plain text files and trick Java into thinking they are coming from the keyboard. Here are step-by-step instructions:

1. Make sure you can compile and run the `Convert.java` example in the `ch03` directory of `ThinkJavaCode`.

2. In the same directory as `Convert.java`, create a plain text file named `test.in` ("in" is for input). Enter the following line and save the file:

   ```
   193.04
   ```

3. Create a second plain text file named `test.exp` ("exp" is for expected). Enter the following line and save the file:

   ```
   193.04 cm = 6 ft, 4 in
   ```

4. Open a terminal, and change to the directory with these files. Run the following command to test the program:

   ```
   java Convert < test.in > test.out
   ```

On the command line, < and > are **redirection operators**. The first one redirects the contents of `test.in` to `System.in`, as if it were entered from the keyboard. The second one redirects the contents of `System.out` to a new file `test.out`, much like a screen capture. In other words, the `test.out` file contains the output of your program.

By the way, it's perfectly okay to compile your programs in DrJava (or some other environment) and run them from the command line. Knowing both techniques allows you to use the right tool for the job.

At this point, we just need to compare the contents `test.out` with `test.exp`. If the files are the same, then the program outputted what we expected it to output. If not, then we found a bug, and we can use the output to begin debugging our program. Fortunately, there's a simple way to compare files on the command line:

```
diff test.exp test.out
```

The `diff` utility summarizes the differences between two files. If there are no differences, then it displays nothing, which in our case is what we want. If the expected output differs from the actual output, then we need to continue debugging. Usually the program is at fault, and `diff` provides some insight about what is broken. But there's also a chance that we have a correct program and the expected output is wrong.

Interpreting the results from `diff` can be confusing, but fortunately there are many graphical tools that show the differences between two files. For example, on Windows you can install `WinMerge`, on Mac you can use `opendiff` (which comes with Xcode), and on Linux there's `meld`, shown in Figure A-4.

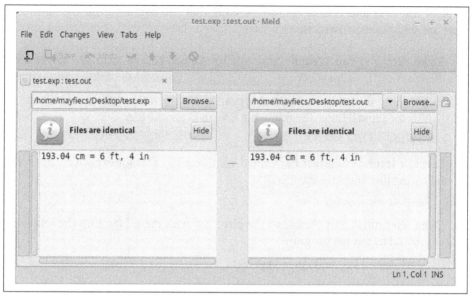

Figure A-4. Using meld *to compare expected output with the actual output.*

Regardless of what tool you use, the goal is the same. Debug your program until the actual output is *identical* to the expected output.

Running Checkstyle

Checkstyle is a command-line tool that can be used to determine if your source code follows a set of style rules. It also checks for common programming mistakes, such as class and method design problems.

You can download the latest version as a JAR file from *http://checkstyle.source forge.net/*. To run Checkstyle, move (or copy) the JAR file to the same directory as your program. Open a terminal in that location, and run the following command:

```
java -jar checkstyle-*-all.jar -c /google_checks.xml *.java
```

The * characters are **wildcards** that match whatever version of Checkstyle you have and whatever Java source files are present. The output indicates the file and line number of each problem. This example refers to a method beginning on line 93, column 5 of Hello.java:

```
Hello.java:93:5: Missing a Javadoc comment
```

The file /google_checks.xml is inside the JAR file and represents most of Google's style rules. You can alternatively use /sun_checks.xml or provide your own configuration file. See Checkstyle's website for more information.

If you apply Checkstyle to your source code often, you will likely internalize good style habits over time. But there are limits to what automatic style checkers can do. In particular, they can't evaluate the *quality* of your comments, the *meaning* of your variable names, or the *structure* of your algorithms.

Good comments make it easier for experienced developers to identify errors in your code. Good variable names communicate the intent of your program and how the data is organized. And good programs are designed to be efficient and demonstrably correct.

Tracing with a Debugger

A great way to visualize the flow of execution, including how parameters and arguments work, is to use a **debugger**. Most debuggers make it possible to:

1. Set a **breakpoint**, a line where you want the program to pause.
2. Step through the code one line at a time and watch what it does.
3. Check the values of variables and see when and how they change.

For example, open any program in DrJava and move the cursor to the first line of main. Press *Ctrl+B* to toggle a breakpoint on the current line; it should now be highlighted in red. Press *Ctrl+Shift+D* to turn on Debug Mode; a new pane should appear at the bottom of the window. These commands are also available from the *Debugger* menu, in case you forget the shortcut keys.

When you run the program, execution pauses at the first breakpoint. The debug pane displays the **call stack**, with the current method on top of the stack, as shown in Figure A-5. You might be surprised to see how many methods were called before the main method!

To the right are several buttons that allow you to step through the code at your own pace. You can also press *Automatic Trace* to watch DrJava run your code one line at a time.

Using a debugger is like having the computer proofread your code out loud. When the program is paused, you can examine (or even change) the value of any variable using the Interactions Pane.

Tracing allows you to follow the flow of execution and see how data pass from one method to another. You might expect the code do one thing, but then the debugger shows it doing something else. At that moment, you gain insight about what may be wrong with the code.

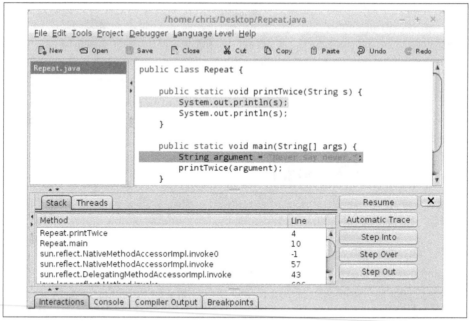

Figure A-5. Screenshot of the DrJava debugger. Execution is currently paused on the first line of printTwice. *There is a breakpoint on the first line of* main.

You can edit your code while debugging it, but we don't recommend it. If you add or delete multiple lines of code while the program is paused, the results can be confusing.

See *http://drjava.org/docs/user/ch09.html* for more information about using the debugger feature of DrJava.

Testing with JUnit

When beginners start writing methods, they usually test them by invoking them from main and checking the results by hand. Writing code like this can get repetitive, but there are tools to make it easier. For cases where we know the right answer, we can do better by writing **unit tests**.

For example, to test fibonacci from "One More Example" on page 82, we could write:

```
public static void main(String[] args) {
    if (fibonacci(1) != 1) {
        System.err.println("fibonacci(1) is incorrect");
    }
    if (fibonacci(2) != 1) {
        System.err.println("fibonacci(2) is incorrect");
    }
```

```
        if (fibonacci(3) != 2) {
            System.err.println("fibonacci(3) is incorrect");
        }
    }
```

This test code is self-explanatory, but it's longer than it needs to be and it doesn't scale very well. In addition, the error messages provide limited information. Using a unit test framework addresses these and other issues.

JUnit is a common testing tool for Java programs (see *http://junit.org*). To use it, you have to create a test class that contains test methods. If the name of your class is Class, the name of the test class is ClassTest. And if there is a method in Class named method, there should be a method in TestClass named testMethod.

For example, suppose that the fibonacci method belongs to a class named Series. Here is the corresponding JUnit test class and test method:

```
import junit.framework.TestCase;

public class SeriesTest extends TestCase {

    public void testFibonacci() {
        assertEquals(1, Series.fibonacci(1));
        assertEquals(1, Series.fibonacci(2));
        assertEquals(2, Series.fibonacci(3));
    }
}
```

This example uses the keyword extends, which indicates that the new class, SeriesTest, is based on an existing class, TestCase, which is imported from the package junit.framework.

Many development environments can generate test classes and test methods automatically. In DrJava, you can select *New JUnit Test Case* from the *File* menu to generate an empty test class.

assertEquals is provided by the TestCase class. It takes two arguments and checks whether they are equal. If so, it does nothing; otherwise it displays a detailed error message. Normally the first argument is the "expected value", which we consider correct, and the second argument is the "actual value" we want to check. If they are not equal, the test fails.

Using assertEquals is more concise than writing your own if statements and Sys tem.err messages. JUnit provides additional assert methods, such as assertNull, assertSame, and assertTrue, that can be used to design a variety of tests.

To run JUnit directly from DrJava, click the *Test* button on the toolbar. If all your test methods pass, you will see a green bar in the lower-right corner. Otherwise, DrJava will take you directly to the first assertion that failed.

Vocabulary

IDE:

An "integrated development environment" that includes tools for editing, compiling, and debugging programs.

JDK:

The "Java Development Kit" that contains the compiler, Javadoc, and other tools.

JVM:

The "Java Virtual Machine" that interprets the compiled byte code.

text editor:

A program that edits plain text files, the format used by most programming languages.

JAR:

A "Java Archive", which is essentially a ZIP file containing classes and other resources.

command-line interface:

A means of interacting with the computer by issuing commands in the form of successive lines of text.

redirection operator:

A command-line feature that substitutes `System.in` and/or `System.out` with a plain text file.

wildcard:

A command-line feature that allows you to specify a pattern of filenames using the * character.

debugger:

A tool that allows you to run one statement at a time and see the contents of variables.

breakpoint:

A line of code where the debugger will pause a running program.

call stack:

The history of method calls and where to resume execution after each method returns.

unit test:

Code that exercises a single method of a program, testing for correctness and/or efficiency.

Java 2D Graphics

The Java library includes a simple package for drawing 2D graphics, called java.awt. **AWT** stands for "Abstract Window Toolkit". We are only going to scratch the surface of graphics programming; you can read more about it in the Java tutorials at *https:// docs.oracle.com/javase/tutorial/2d/*.

Creating Graphics

There are several ways to create graphics in Java; the simplest way is to use java.awt.Canvas and java.awt.Graphics. A Canvas is a blank rectangular area of the screen onto which the application can draw. The Graphics class provides basic drawing methods such as drawLine, drawRect, and drawString.

Here is an example program that draws a circle using the fillOval method:

```
import java.awt.Canvas;
import java.awt.Graphics;
import javax.swing.JFrame;

public class Drawing extends Canvas {

    public static void main(String[] args) {
        JFrame frame = new JFrame("My Drawing");
        Canvas canvas = new Drawing();
        canvas.setSize(400, 400);
        frame.add(canvas);
        frame.pack();
        frame.setVisible(true);
    }

    public void paint(Graphics g) {
        g.fillOval(100, 100, 200, 200);
    }
}
```

The Drawing class extends Canvas, so it has all the methods provided by Canvas, including setSize. You can read about the other methods in the documentation, which you can find by doing a web search for "Java Canvas".

In the main method, we:

1. Create a JFrame object, which is the window that will contain the canvas.

2. Create a Drawing object (which is the canvas), set its width and height, and add it to the frame.

3. Pack the frame (resize it) to fit the canvas, and display it on the screen.

Once the frame is visible, the paint method is called whenever the canvas needs to be drawn; for example, when the window is moved or resized. The application doesn't end after the main method returns; instead, it waits for the JFrame to close. If you run this code, you should see a black circle on a gray background.

Graphics Methods

You are probably used to Cartesian **coordinates**, where *x* and *y* values can be positive or negative. In contrast, Java uses a coordinate system where the origin is in the upper-left corner. That way, *x* and *y* are always positive integers. Figure B-1 shows these coordinate systems.

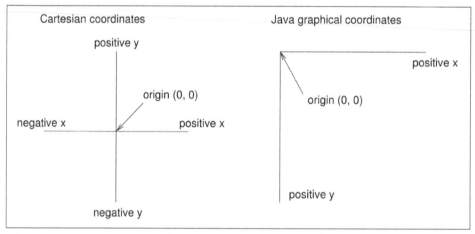

Figure B-1. Diagram of the difference between Cartesian coordinates and Java graphical coordinates.

Graphical coordinates are measured in **pixels**; each pixel corresponds to a dot on the screen.

To draw on the canvas, you invoke methods on a Graphics object. You don't have to create the Graphics object; it gets created when you create the Canvas, and it gets passed as an argument to paint.

The previous example used fillOval, which has the following signature:

```
/**
 * Fills an oval bounded by the specified rectangle with
 * the current color.
 */
public void fillOval(int x, int y, int width, int height)
```

The four parameters specify a **bounding box**, which is the rectangle in which the oval is drawn. x and y specify the the location of the upper-left corner of the bounding box. The bounding box itself is not drawn (see Figure B-2).

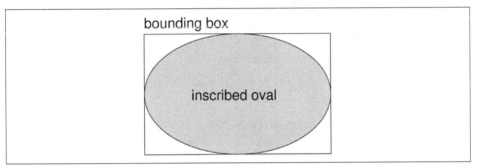

Figure B-2. Diagram of an oval inside its bounding box.

To choose the color of a shape, invoke setColor on the Graphics object:

```
g.setColor(Color.red);
```

The setColor method determines the color of everything that gets drawn afterward. Color.red is a constant provided by the Color class; to use it you have to import java.awt.Color. Other colors include:

```
black       blue      cyan      darkGray    gray     green
lightGray   magenta   orange    pink        white    yellow
```

You can create your own colors by specifying the red, green, and blue (**RGB**) components. For example:

```
Color purple = new Color(128, 0, 128);
```

Each value is an integer in the range 0 (darkest) to 255 (lightest). The color (0, 0, 0) is black, and (255, 255, 255) is white.

You can set the background color of the Canvas by invoking setBackground:

```
canvas.setBackground(Color.white);
```

Example Drawing

Suppose we want to draw a "Hidden Mickey", which is an icon that represents Mickey Mouse (see *https://en.wikipedia.org/wiki/Hidden_Mickey*). We can use the oval we just drew as the face, and then add two ears. To make the code more readable, let's use Rectangle objects to represent bounding boxes.

Here's a method that takes a Rectangle and invokes fillOval:

```
public void boxOval(Graphics g, Rectangle bb) {
    g.fillOval(bb.x, bb.y, bb.width, bb.height);
}
```

And here's a method that draws Mickey Mouse:

```
public void mickey(Graphics g, Rectangle bb) {
    boxOval(g, bb);

    int dx = bb.width / 2;
    int dy = bb.height / 2;
    Rectangle half = new Rectangle(bb.x, bb.y, dx, dy);

    half.translate(-dx / 2, -dy / 2);
    boxOval(g, half);

    half.translate(dx * 2, 0);
    boxOval(g, half);
}
```

The first line draws the face. The next three lines create a smaller rectangle for the ears. We translate the rectangle up and left for the first ear, then to the right for the second ear. The result is shown in Figure B-3.

Figure B-3. A "Hidden Mickey" drawn using Java graphics.

You can read more about Rectangle and translate in Chapter 10. See the exercises at the end of this appendix for more example drawings.

Vocabulary

AWT:
> The "Abstract Window Toolkit", a Java package for creating graphical user interfaces.

coordinate:
> A value that specifies a location in a two-dimensional graphical window.

pixel:
> The unit in which coordinates are measured.

bounding box:
> A common way to specify the coordinates of a rectangular area.

RGB:
> A color model based on adding red, green, and blue light.

Exercises

The code for this chapter is in the `ap02` directory of `ThinkJavaCode`. See "Using the Code Examples" on page xi for instructions on how to download the repository. Before you start the exercises, we recommend that you compile and run the examples.

Exercise B-1.

Draw the flag of Japan: a red circle on a white background that is wider than it is tall.

Exercise B-2.

Modify `Mickey.java` to draw ears on the ears, and ears on those ears, and more ears all the way down until the smallest ears are only 3 pixels wide.

The result should look like "Mickey Moose", shown in Figure B-4. *Hint:* You should only have to add or modify a few lines of code.

Figure B-4. A recursive shape we call "Mickey Moose".

Exercise B-3.

In this exercise, you will draw "Moiré patterns" that seem to shift around as you move. For an explanation of what is going on, see *https://en.wikipedia.org/wiki/Moire_pattern*.

1. In the directory app02 in the repository for this book, you'll find a file named Moire.java. Open it and read the paint method. Draw a sketch of what you expect it to do. Now run it. Did you get what you expected?

2. Modify the program so that the space between the circles is larger or smaller. See what happens to the image.

3. Modify the program so that the circles are drawn in the center of the screen and concentric, as in Figure B-5 (left). The distance between the circles should be small enough that the Moiré interference is apparent.

4. Write a method named radial that draws a radial set of line segments as shown in Figure B-5 (right), but they should be close enough together to create a Moiré pattern.

5. Just about any kind of graphical pattern can generate Moiré-like interference patterns. Play around and see what you can create.

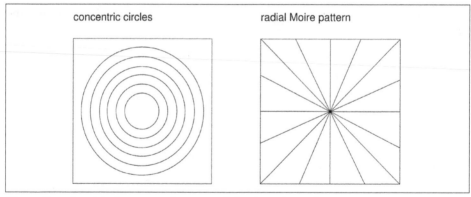

Figure B-5. Graphical patterns that can exhibit Moiré interference.

Debugging

Although there are debugging suggestions throughout the book, we thought it would be useful to organize them in an appendix. If you are having a hard time debugging, you might want to review this appendix from time to time.

The best debugging strategy depends on what kind of error you have:

- **Compile-time errors** indicate that there is something wrong with the syntax of the program. Example: omitting the semicolon at the end of a statement.
- **Run-time errors** are produced if something goes wrong while the program is running. Example: infinite recursion eventually causes a `StackOverflowError`.
- **Logic errors** cause the program to do the wrong thing. Example: an expression may not be evaluated in the order you expect.

The following sections are organized by error type; some techniques are useful for more than one type.

Compile-Time Errors

The best kind of debugging is the kind you don't have to do because you avoid making errors in the first place. Incremental development, which we presented in "Writing Methods" on page 73, can help. The key is to start with a working program and add small amounts of code at a time. When there is an error, you will have a pretty good idea where it is.

Nevertheless, you might find yourself in one of the following situations. For each situation, we have some suggestions about how to proceed.

The compiler is spewing error messages.

If the compiler reports 100 error messages, that doesn't mean there are 100 errors in your program. When the compiler encounters an error, it often gets thrown off track for a while. It tries to recover and pick up again after the first error, but sometimes it reports spurious errors.

Only the first error message is truly reliable. We suggest that you only fix one error at a time, and then recompile the program. You may find that one semicolon or brace "fixes" 100 errors.

I'm getting a weird compiler message, and it won't go away.

First of all, read the error message carefully. It may be written in terse jargon, but often there is a carefully hidden kernel of information.

If nothing else, the message will tell you where in the program the problem occurred. Actually, it tells you where the compiler was when it noticed a problem, which is not necessarily where the error is. Use the information the compiler gives you as a guideline, but if you don't see an error where the compiler is pointing, broaden the search.

Generally the error will be prior to the location of the error message, but there are cases where it will be somewhere else entirely. For example, if you get an error message at a method invocation, the actual error may be in the method definition itself.

If you don't find the error quickly, take a breath and look more broadly at the entire program. Make sure the program is indented properly; that makes it easier to spot syntax errors.

Now, start looking for common syntax errors:

1. Check that all parentheses and brackets are balanced and properly nested. All method definitions should be nested within a class definition. All program statements should be within a method definition.

2. Remember that uppercase letters are not the same as lowercase letters.

3. Check for semicolons at the end of statements (and no semicolons after squiggly braces).

4. Make sure that any strings in the code have matching quotation marks. Make sure that you use double quotes for strings and single quotes for characters.

5. For each assignment statement, make sure that the type on the left is the same as the type on the right. Make sure that the expression on the left is a variable name or something else that you can assign a value to (like an element of an array).

6. For each method invocation, make sure that the arguments you provide are in the right order and have the right type, and that the object you are invoking the method on is the right type.

7. If you are invoking a value method, make sure you are doing something with the result. If you are invoking a void method, make sure you are *not* trying to do something with the result.

8. If you are invoking an instance method, make sure you are invoking it on an object with the right type. If you are invoking a static method from outside the class where it is defined, make sure you specify the class name (using dot notation).

9. Inside an instance method you can refer to the instance variables without specifying an object. If you try that in a static method—with or without `this`—you get a message like "non-static variable x cannot be referenced from a static context."

If nothing works, move on to the next section...

I can't get my program to compile no matter what I do.

If the compiler says there is an error and you don't see it, that might be because you and the compiler are not looking at the same code. Check your development environment to make sure the program you are editing is the program the compiler is compiling.

This situation is often the result of having multiple copies of the same program. You might be editing one version of the file, but compiling a different version.

If you are not sure, try putting an obvious and deliberate syntax error right at the beginning of the program. Now compile again. If the compiler doesn't find the new error, there is probably something wrong with the way you set up the development environment.

If you have examined the code thoroughly, and you are sure the compiler is compiling the right source file, it is time for desperate measures: **debugging by bisection**.

- Make a backup of the file you are working on. If you are working on `Bob.java`, make a copy called `Bob.java.old`.

- Delete about half the code from `Bob.java`. Try compiling again.
  - If the program compiles now, you know the error is in the code you deleted. Bring back about half of what you deleted and repeat.
  - If the program still doesn't compile, the error must be in the code that remains. Delete about half of the remaining code and repeat.

- Once you have found and fixed the error, start bringing back the code you deleted, a little bit at a time.

This process is ugly, but it goes faster than you might think, and it is very reliable. It works for other programming languages too!

I did what the compiler told me to do, but it still doesn't work.

Some error messages come with tidbits of advice, like "class Golfer must be declared abstract. It does not define int compareTo(java.lang.Object) from interface java.lang.Comparable." It sounds like the compiler is telling you to declare `Golfer` as an `abstract` class, and if you are reading this book, you probably don't know what that is or how to do it.

Fortunately, the compiler is wrong. The solution in this case is to make sure `Golfer` has a method called `compareTo` that takes an `Object` as a parameter.

Don't let the compiler lead you by the nose. Error messages give you evidence that something is wrong, but the remedies they suggest are unreliable.

Run-Time Errors

It's not always clear what causes a run-time error, but you can often figure things out by adding print statements to your program.

My program hangs.

If a program stops and seems to be doing nothing, we say it is "hanging". Often that means it is caught in an infinite loop or an infinite recursion.

- If there is a particular loop that you suspect is the problem, add a print statement immediately before the loop that says "entering the loop" and another immediately after that says "exiting the loop".

  Run the program. If you get the first message and not the second, you know where the program is getting stuck. Go to the section titled "Infinite loop".

- Most of the time an infinite recursion will cause the program to run for a while and then produce a `StackOverflowError`. If that happens, go to the section titled "Infinite recursion".

  If you are not getting a `StackOverflowError`, but you suspect there is a problem with a recursive method, you can still use the techniques in the infinite recursion section.

- If neither of the previous suggestions helps, you might not understand the flow of execution in your program. Go to the section titled "Flow of execution".

Infinite loop

If you think you have an infinite loop and you know which loop it is, add a print statement at the end of the loop that displays the values of the variables in the condition, and the value of the condition.

For example:

```
while (x > 0 && y < 0) {
    // do something to x
    // do something to y

    System.out.println("x: " + x);
    System.out.println("y: " + y);
    System.out.println("condition: " + (x > 0 && y < 0));
}
```

Now when you run the program you see three lines of output for each time through the loop. The last time through the loop, the condition should be false. If the loop keeps going, you will see the values of x and y, and you might figure out why they are not getting updated correctly.

Infinite recursion

Most of the time, an infinite recursion will cause the program to throw a StackOverflowError. But if the program is slow, it may take a long time to fill the stack.

If you know which method is causing an infinite recursion, check that there is a base case. There should be some condition that makes the method return without making a recursive invocation. If not, you need to rethink the algorithm and identify a base case.

If there is a base case, but the program doesn't seem to be reaching it, add a print statement at the beginning of the method that displays the parameters. Now when you run the program you see a few lines of output every time the method is invoked, and you can see the values of the parameters. If the parameters are not moving toward the base case, you might see why not.

Flow of execution

If you are not sure how the flow of execution is moving through your program, add print statements to the beginning of each method with a message like "entering method foo", where foo is the name of the method. Now when you run the program, it displays a trace of each method as it is invoked.

You can also display the arguments each method receives. When you run the program, check whether the values are reasonable, and check for one of the most common errors—providing arguments in the wrong order.

When I run the program I get an exception.

When an exception occurs, Java displays a message that includes the name of the exception, the line of the program where the exception occurred, and a "stack trace". The stack trace includes the method that was running, the method that invoked it, the method that invoked that one, and so on.

The first step is to examine the place in the program where the error occurred and see if you can figure out what happened.

NullPointerException:
> You tried to access an instance variable or invoke a method on an object that is currently null. You should figure out which variable is null and then figure out how it got to be that way.
>
> Remember that when you declare a variable with an array type, its elements are initially null until you assign a value to them. For example, this code causes a NullPointerException:

```
int[] array = new Point[5];
System.out.println(array[0].x);
```

ArrayIndexOutOfBoundsException:
> The index you are using to access an array is either negative or greater than array.length - 1. If you can find the site where the problem is, add a print statement immediately before it to display the value of the index and the length of the array. Is the array the right size? Is the index the right value?
>
> Now work your way backwards through the program and see where the array and the index come from. Find the nearest assignment statement and see if it is doing the right thing. If either one is a parameter, go to the place where the method is invoked and see where the values are coming from.

StackOverflowError:
> See "Infinite recursion" on page 221.

FileNotFoundException:
> This means Java didn't find the file it was looking for. If you are using a project-based development environment like Eclipse, you might have to import the file

into the project. Otherwise make sure the file exists and that the path is correct. This problem depends on your file system, so it can be hard to track down.

ArithmeticException:
Something went wrong during an arithmetic operation; for example, division by zero.

I added so many print statements I get inundated with output.

One of the problems with using print statements for debugging is that you can end up buried in output. There are two ways to proceed: either simplify the output, or simplify the program.

To simplify the output, you can remove or comment out print statements that aren't helping, or combine them, or format the output so it is easier to understand. As you develop a program, you should write code to generate concise, informative traces of what the program is doing.

To simplify the program, scale down the problem the program is working on. For example, if you are sorting an array, sort a *small* array. If the program takes input from the user, give it the simplest input that causes the error.

Also, clean up the code. Remove unnecessary or experimental parts, and reorganize the program to make it easier to read. For example, if you suspect that the error is in a deeply-nested part of the program, rewrite that part with a simpler structure. If you suspect a large method, split it into smaller methods and test them separately.

The process of finding the minimal test case often leads you to the bug. For example, if you find that a program works when the array has an even number of elements, but not when it has an odd number, that gives you a clue about what is going on.

Reorganizing the program can help you find subtle bugs. If you make a change that you think doesn't affect the program, and it does, that can tip you off.

Logic Errors

My program doesn't work.

Logic errors are hard to find because the compiler and interpreter provide no information about what is wrong. Only you know what the program is supposed to do, and only you know that it isn't doing it.

The first step is to make a connection between the code and the behavior you get. You need a hypothesis about what the program is actually doing. Here are some questions to ask yourself:

- Is there something the program was supposed to do, but doesn't seem to be happening? Find the section of the code that performs that function, and make sure it is executing when you think it should. See "Flow of execution" on page 221.

- Is something happening that shouldn't? Find code in your program that performs that function, and see if it is executing when it shouldn't.

- Is a section of code producing an unexpected effect? Make sure you understand the code, especially if it invokes methods in the Java library. Read the documentation for those methods, and try them out with simple test cases. They might not do what you think they do.

To program, you need a mental model of what your code does. If it doesn't do what you expect, the problem might not actually be the program; it might be in your head.

The best way to correct your mental model is to break the program into components (usually the classes and methods) and test them independently. Once you find the discrepancy between your model and reality, you can solve the problem.

Here are some common logic errors to check for:

- Remember that integer division always rounds toward zero. If you want fractions, use `double`. More generally, use integers for countable things and floating-point numbers for measurable things.

- Floating-point numbers are only approximate, so don't rely on them to be perfectly accurate. You should probably never use the `==` operator with `doubles`. Instead of writing `if (d == 1.23)`, do something like `if (Math.abs(d - 1.23) < .000001)`.

- When you apply the equality operator (`==`) to objects, it checks whether they are identical. If you meant to check equivalence, you should use the `equals` method instead.

- By default for user-defined types, `equals` checks identity. If you want a different notion of equivalence, you have to override it.

- Inheritance can lead to subtle logic errors, because you can run inherited code without realizing it. See "Flow of execution" on page 221.

I've got a big hairy expression and it doesn't do what I expect.

Writing complex expressions is fine as long as they are readable, but they can be hard to debug. It is often a good idea to break a complex expression into a series of assignments to temporary variables.

```
rect.setLocation(rect.getLocation().translate(
                -rect.getWidth(), -rect.getHeight()));
```

This example can be rewritten as:

```
int dx = -rect.getWidth();
int dy = -rect.getHeight();
Point location = rect.getLocation();
Point newLocation = location.translate(dx, dy);
rect.setLocation(newLocation);
```

The second version is easier to read, partly because the variable names provide additional documentation. It's also easier to debug, because you can check the types of the temporary variables and display their values.

Another problem that can occur with big expressions is that the order of operations may not be what you expect. For example, to evaluate $\frac{x}{2\pi}$, you might write:

```
double y = x / 2 * Math.PI;
```

That is not correct, because multiplication and division have the same precedence, and they are evaluated from left to right. This code computes $\frac{x}{2}\pi$.

If you are not sure of the order of operations, check the documentation, or use parentheses to make it explicit.

```
double y = x / (2 * Math.PI);
```

This version is correct, and more readable for other people who haven't memorized the order of operations.

My method doesn't return what I expect.

If you have a return statement with a complex expression, you don't have a chance to display the value before returning.

```
public Rectangle intersection(Rectangle a, Rectangle b) {
    return new Rectangle(
        Math.min(a.x, b.x), Math.min(a.y, b.y),
        Math.max(a.x + a.width, b.x + b.width)
            - Math.min(a.x, b.x)
        Math.max(a.y + a.height, b.y + b.height)
            - Math.min(a.y, b.y));
}
```

Instead of writing everything in one statement, use temporary variables:

```
public Rectangle intersection(Rectangle a, Rectangle b) {
    int x1 = Math.min(a.x, b.x);
    int y1 = Math.min(a.y, b.y);
    int x2 = Math.max(a.x + a.width, b.x + b.width);
    int y2 = Math.max(a.y + a.height, b.y + b.height);
    Rectangle rect = new Rectangle(x1, y1, x2 - x1, y2 - y1);
    return rect;
}
```

Now you have the opportunity to display any of the intermediate variables before returning. And by reusing x1 and y1, you made the code smaller, too.

My print statement isn't doing anything.

If you use the `println` method, the output is displayed immediately, but if you use `print` (at least in some environments), the output gets stored without being displayed until the next newline. If the program terminates without displaying a newline, you may never see the stored output. If you suspect that this is happening, change some or all of the `print` statements to `println`.

I'm really, really stuck and I need help.

First, get away from the computer for a few minutes. Computers emit waves that affect the brain, causing the following symptoms:

- Frustration and rage.
- Superstitious beliefs ("the computer hates me") and magical thinking ("the program only works when I wear my hat backwards").
- Sour grapes ("this program is lame anyway").

If you suffer from any of these symptoms, get up and go for a walk. When you are calm, think about the program. What is it doing? What are possible causes of that behavior? When was the last time you had a working program, and what did you do next?

Sometimes it just takes time to find a bug. People often find bugs when they let their mind wander. Good places to find bugs are buses, showers, and bed.

No, I really need help.

It happens. Even the best programmers get stuck. Sometimes you need a another pair of eyes.

Before you bring someone else in, make sure you have tried the techniques described in this appendix.

Your program should be as simple as possible, and you should be working on the smallest input that causes the error. You should have print statements in the appropriate places (and the output they produce should be comprehensible). You should understand the problem well enough to describe it concisely.

When you bring someone in to help, give them the information they need:

- What kind of bug is it? Compile-time, run-time, or logic?
- What was the last thing you did before this error occurred? What were the last lines of code that you wrote, or what is the test case that fails?
- If the bug occurs at compile time or run time, what is the error message, and what part of the program does it indicate?
- What have you tried, and what have you learned?

By the time you explain the problem to someone, you might see the answer. This phenomenon is so common that some people recommend a debugging technique called "rubber ducking". Here's how it works:

1. Buy a standard-issue rubber duck.
2. When you are really stuck on a problem, put the rubber duck on the desk in front of you and say, "Rubber duck, I am stuck on a problem. Here's what's happening..."
3. Explain the problem to the rubber duck.
4. Discover the solution.
5. Thank the rubber duck.

We're not kidding, it works! See *https://en.wikipedia.org/wiki/Rubber_duck_debugging*.

I found the bug!

When you find the bug, it is usually obvious how to fix it. But not always. Sometimes what seems to be a bug is really an indication that you don't understand the program, or there is an error in your algorithm. In these cases, you might have to rethink the algorithm, or adjust your mental model. Take some time away from the computer to think, work through test cases by hand, or draw diagrams to represent the computation.

After you fix the bug, don't just start in making new errors. Take a minute to think about what kind of bug it was, why you made the error, how the error manifested itself, and what you could have done to find it faster. Next time you see something similar, you will be able to find the bug more quickly. Or even better, you will learn to avoid that type of bug for good.

Index

definition, 4, 145
Graphics, 211
JFrame, 212
Math, 43
Point, 131
Rectangle, 133
Scanner, 30
System, 29
Time, 146
utility, 30
class diagram, 138, 140
class variable, 164, 172
client, 149, 156
collection, 186
Color, 213
command-line interface, 203, 210
comment, 10
documentation, 53
inline, 5
comparable, 166
compareTo, 121
comparison operator, 57
compile, 3, 9, 218
compile-time error, 21, 25, 217
complete ordering, 165
composition, 21, 25, 44, 75
computer science, 2, 9
concatenate, 20, 25, 125
conditional statement, 59, 66
constant, 33, 39
constructor, 146, 156, 162, 175, 179
value, 148
continue, 98
coordinate, 212, 215
counter, 109
Crazy Eights, 185

D

data encapsulation, 145, 156
De Morgan's laws, 58, 66
dead code, 73, 82
debugger, 207, 210
debugging, 2, 9, 217
by bisection, 219
experimental, 8
rubber duck, 227
declaration, 13, 24, 132
decrement, 97, 99
degrees, 43

dependent, 150
deterministic, 108, 112
diagram
class, 138
stack, 50, 64, 80
state, 15, 104, 132
divisible, 36
division
floating-point, 91
integer, 17, 18
do-while, 97
documentation, 51, 55, 139
Javadoc comments, 53
Javadoc tags, 78
dot notation, 132, 140
double, 17
Double, 123
doubloon, 129
DrJava, 201

E

efficiency, 101, 111, 169, 178, 183, 187
element, 103, 104, 112
empty array, 124, 125
empty string, 120, 125
encapsulate, 92, 99
encapsulation, 126, 135
data, 145
encode, 162
enhanced for loop, 111, 112
equals, 121, 152, 153
equivalent, 152, 157, 165
error
compile-time, 21, 217
logic, 23, 217, 224
message, 8, 21, 21, 218
run-time, 22, 217
syntax, 218
escape sequence, 6, 10, 118
exception, 22, 217, 222
Arithmetic, 23
ArrayIndexOutOfBounds, 105
InputMismatch, 62
NegativeArraySize, 104
NullPointer, 137, 167
StackOverflow, 172
StringIndexOutOfBounds, 119
executable, 3, 10
experimental debugging, 8

expression, 17, 24, 43, 44
  big and hairy, 224
  boolean, 61
extends, 186, 189
extract digits, 36

F

factorial, 79, 83, 143
fibonacci, 82
FileNotFoundException, 222
final, 33, 92, 165, 167
flag, 61, 67
floating-point, 17, 25
flow of execution, 47, 54, 221
for, 96
format specifier, 34, 39
format string, 34, 39, 151
frame, 50, 54
functional decomposition, 76, 83

G

garbage collection, 138, 140
generalization, 93, 94, 126, 135
generalize, 92, 99
getter, 150, 157
GitHub, xi
Google style, 7
Graphics, 211
Greenfield, Larry, 8

H

hanging, 220
HAS-A, 197, 198
hello world, 4
helper method, 177, 181
hexadecimal, 29, 151
high-level language, 3, 9
histogram, 109, 112, 173
HTML, 53, 78, 139

I

IDE, 201
identical, 157
if statement, 59
immutable, 118, 125, 156, 166
import statement, 30, 38
increment, 97, 99
incremental development, 73, 82

independent, 150
index, 104, 112, 168
indexOf, 121
infinite loop, 90, 99, 220
infinite recursion, 148, 172, 220, 221
information hiding, 146, 156
inheritance, 186, 197, 198
initialize, 15, 24, 61
InputMismatchException, 62
instance, 145, 156
instance method, 152, 154, 157
instance variable, 146, 156
instantiate, 145, 156
Integer, 123
integer division, 17, 18
interpret, 3, 9
invoke, 43, 54
IS-A, 197, 198
iteration, 89

J

JAR, 202, 210
java.awt, 131
java.util, 30
Javadoc, 53, 55, 78, 139, 201
JDK, 201, 210
JFrame, 212
JVM, 3, 201, 210

K

keyword, 14, 24, 147

L

language
  complete, 79
  high-level, 3
  low-level, 3
leap of faith, 81, 83, 181
length
  array, 107
  string, 119
library, 29, 38, 139
Linux, 8
literal, 33, 39
local variable, 49, 54
logarithm, 62, 90
logic error, 23, 25, 217, 224
logical operator, 58, 66, 165

suit, 161
super, 189
superclass, 189, 198
syntax, 14, 24, 217
syntax errors, 218
System.err, 62, 98, 209
System.in, 30, 117, 205
System.out, 29, 117, 205

T

table, 90
    two-dimensional, 92
tag, 78, 83
temporary variable, 72, 82, 225
terminal, 203
testing, 182
text editor, 201, 210
this, 147, 187
Time, 146
    addition, 154
toCharArray, 119
token, 31, 39
toLowerCase, 118
top-down development, 177, 181, 192, 194
Torvalds, Linus, 8
toString, 151
toUpperCase, 118
traversal, 107, 112
traverse, 119, 169
Turing complete, 79, 83
Turing, Alan, 79, 118
type, 24
    array, 103
    boolean, 57
    char, 13, 117
    double, 17

int, 13
long, 19, 44
object, 145
String, 5, 13, 131
void, 45
type cast, 35, 39

U

UML, 138, 140, 197
Unicode, 118, 125
unit test, 208, 210
utility class, 30, 106
utility method, 122

V

value, 13, 24
value constructor, 148
value method, 71, 72, 82
variable, 13
    instance, 146
    local, 49
    loop, 93, 105, 119
    private, 146, 149
    static, 164
    temporary, 72, 225
virtual machine, 3, 201
void, 45, 71
void method, 71

W

while, 89
wildcard, 206, 210
wrapper class, 123, 125
wrapper method, 188, 198

About the Authors

Allen Downey is a Professor of Computer Science at Olin College of Engineering. He has taught computer science at Wellesley College, Colby College and U.C. Berkeley. He has a Ph.D. in Computer Science from U.C. Berkeley and Master's and Bachelor's degrees from MIT.

Chris Mayfield is an Associate Professor of Computer Science at James Madison University, with a research focus on CS education and professional development. He has a Ph.D. in Computer Science from Purdue University and Bachelor's degrees in CS and German from the University of Utah.

Colophon

The animal on the cover of *Think Java* is a red-tailed black cockatoo (*Calyptorhynchus banksii*), also known as Banks' black cockatoo after an 18th-century English botanist. It is a large bird native to Australia, found in many habitats such as forests, open plains, or riverlands, often nesting in eucalyptus trees.

As suggested by their name, these birds have black plumage, though only males have vivid red panels on their tails. They are typically around 2 feet in length and weigh between 1–2 pounds. Like other cockatoo species, the red-tailed black cockatoo has a large curved beak, the ability to raise a feathered crest on its head, and feet with 2 toes facing forward and two facing backward. This allows them to grab and manipulate objects with one foot while gripping a branch with the other. Interestingly, the vast majority of cockatoos are left-footed.

The diet of the red-tailed black cockatoo is primarily made up of eucalyptus seeds, though it will also eat nuts, fruits, insects, and various grains. They are very noisy birds, and will flock in large groups near plentiful food sources. However, this species is typically very shy around humans.

Due to their reliance on trees for shelter and food, the red-tailed black cockatoo is sensitive to deforestation, which threatens some populations in southeastern Australia. In addition, while Australia requires a special license to keep and breed these birds, they are still affected by illegal smuggling for the pet trade—they can have long lifespans in captivity and are in high demand.

Many of the animals on O'Reilly covers are endangered; all of them are important to the world. To learn more about how you can help, go to *animals.oreilly.com*.

The cover image is from *Wood's Illustrated Natural History*. The cover fonts are URW Typewriter and Guardian Sans. The text font is Adobe Minion Pro; the heading font is Adobe Myriad Condensed; and the code font is Dalton Maag's Ubuntu Mono.

Learn from experts.
Find the answers you need.

Sign up for a **10-day free trial** to get **unlimited access** to all of the content on Safari, including Learning Paths, interactive tutorials, and curated playlists that draw from thousands of ebooks and training videos on a wide range of topics, including data, design, DevOps, management, business—and much more.

Start your free trial at:

oreilly.com/safari

(No credit card required.)

CPSIA information can be obtained
at www.ICGtesting.com
Printed in the USA
BVHW06s2012060818
523682BV00015B/630/P

9 781491 929568